The
Jewel
Garden

The
Jewel
Garden

Monty and Sarah Don

Special photography by Nicola Browne

Hodder & Stoughton

This book is dedicated
to those who have
helped us make and
maintain this garden:
George and Rose Taylor,
Maureen Turner, Fred
Ellis and Jim Kelly,
Gareth Lorman,
Norman and Jayne
Groves. Their work
shows on every page.

Beginnings

Monty: The jewel garden really began in the spring of 1981, when we started the jewellery business. Sarah and I were living in London, in a rented basement flat just round the corner from the Angel, Islington. The nearest we got to a garden was peering through the locked French windows of our tiny bedroom. Officially I was a postgraduate student at the London School of Economics, but in reality I had dropped out of my course and was biding time as a waiter at Joe Allen's restaurant in Covent Garden. Although it was fun to go from a student's penury to having cash in my pocket, and although I knew that my postgraduate work on Economic History was a sham and therefore any kind of paid work was preferable, I also knew I was wasting time.

From the age of 13, school had been a disaster. I hated the public school I was sent to, they hated me and finally, at 15, they kicked me out. The Basingstoke comprehensive was more friendly but closed its sixth form after I'd been there a year. The sixth-form college that followed had girls and, thrown into a state of erotic astonishment, I did no work at all. I left school at 18 with a meagre batch of terrible 'A' levels. I retook one at night school whilst working as a building labourer, did well, and decided I'd go to Cambridge. So I rang the sixth-form college for advice. They openly jeered at my pretension. I clearly remember the single exclamation of my old tutor – 'You!' I thought, yes, you bugger, me, and I'll do it just to spite you. Perhaps he was canny enough to know how to get the best from me, but I think that's being over-generous. So I got a job on a pig farm in the mornings and spent every afternoon for six months going through old Oxbridge entrance papers. At the age of 21 I was accepted. Older than most of my contemporaries, I was a bit of an outsider, but was taught by a wonderful man, Arthur Sale, who valued and nurtured in me all the things that I wanted to be. I left determined to be a writer.

> *Sarah*: Montagu and I met at Cambridge. He was an undergraduate and my then husband was a postgraduate at the same college. In 1979 I left my well-off husband for this penniless student. Trying to escape the inevitable mess that we had created, Montagu and I ran away together to the North York Moors where we were offered rooms in a house for the winter, so long as we paid the rent by riding the owner's horse every day and painting all the windows. We now look back on that time as a rich experience, but there was real hardship. Montagu was trying to write a novel and helping out on local farms, while I was making jewellery. We were more or less broke.
>
> In early 1980 I started a part-time course in London. We both headed south and, after a spell while Montagu worked as a dustman back in Cambridge – which he loved because he could finish by lunchtime and write in the afternoons – we found rooms in London.

Things seemed to be going wrong. I was 25, with a degree from Cambridge but no qualifications of any kind, I wanted to write but had published nothing, had dropped out of the LSE and was a waiter. Nothing wrong with that as far as it went, but it was not how I had seen my life unfolding. Apart from anything else I was a country boy, and the nocturnal urban life was as far removed from my world and its rhythms as could be imagined.

Then I was hit by a bout of depression that kept me to my bed for a number of weeks. If nothing else – and one of the points about depression is that there *is* nothing else for great spans of muddy time – it gave me time to think. Since leaving school seven years earlier I had done any job going to provide myself with money, usually involving hard physical graft.

From a small boy I had wanted only to be a writer and to work on the land. A hurdle-maker's life seemed to me to be ideal, coppicing your materials with hand tools in the woods and then making hurdles with hypnotic skill. As a student I had seriously considered becoming a thatcher. In an ideal world I would farm as well, but I had worked on farms and seen that only those with money had any chance of owning their land and for me, possession was a large part of the draw. The only writing that I considered was fiction. It never crossed my mind to write about gardening, even though by then I had written – and destroyed – a couple of excruciatingly bad novels, and was facing the sneaking suspicion that I might not be any good at it.

Whilst I was taking stock of my life Sarah was going through the same process.

When I was 19 I married for the first time, and went to live in Papua New Guinea, where my husband was researching the winged bean. During my four years there I collected primitive jewellery and artefacts and ended up with a substantial collection. This was the beginning of my interest in jewellery. I then apprenticed myself to a jeweller called Casty Cobb, who let me work in her house for eighteen months, where I learned all the basic techniques. During this time I also spent four months in Rome studying Etruscan and classical jewellery.

I assembled a collection of tools that would fit into a trunk. I had decided that I would spend my life travelling round the world with my husband and wherever I landed, I could open up the trunk and get to work. However, the marriage collapsed, and I was left with my trunk of tools and Montagu on the North York Moors.

Jewellery

After the bleak isolation of Yorkshire in winter, I enrolled at the Sir John Cass College in Whitechapel and found myself surrounded by 17-year-old apprentices. This was a new and fascinating world for me. Jewellery and silversmithing were divided up into different trades – polishers, finishers, planishers, platers and engravers, each with distinct skills and applications and most working in almost Dickensian conditions in small workshops in an area based around Clerkenwell.

It was at that time – May 1981 – that we bumped into someone Sarah had met through her jewellery class who had a studio in Clerkenwell but was moving. On the spur of the moment we agreed to take it over. Neither of us had any business experience but it felt like a good idea at the time. I threw myself into it with all my energy and enthusiasm. Working with Sarah felt like a natural extension to the rest of our life together. It still does.

I knew that I would never be a great craftsman. I was impatient and the skills took years to gain. So, armed with a basic technical knowledge, we started to make jewellery. We had a box of tools, now we had a workshop, and we had to try and earn a living from them.

Up until this point my training had been in fine jewellery, using gold and silver. But I was increasingly attracted to fashion and costume jewellery, which was essentially fake. Since the Fifties this had rather gone out of fashion. We thought that we would design our jewellery on exactly the same timetable and basis as clothes designers, doing large collections that we would show twice a year in Fashion Week. It was not such a big idea, but no one else was doing it at the time.

Everything had to be learned. The studio was up eight flights of stairs in a building on Old Street and was part of a cooperative. We learned hungrily from all the other members, everything from soldering and polishing to filing systems and how to make out an invoice. Starting a business is intensely exciting. Everything is a challenge, everything has to be done for the first time. It took me a while to learn that running one is profoundly boring.

Selling

Our second studio was above a stable in Islington. Montagu had to muck it out before we could move in.

I spent that winter trudging round London with a suitcase trying to sell the few pieces that we had made to stores, magazines and fashion designers. Most were polite but unresponsive. One buyer kept me waiting for 45 minutes, wouldn't let me sit down, looked at the pieces that I placed on her desk, then straight in

my eyes and said, 'Why did you bother to come here with this *stuff*?' Humiliated, I repacked our precious stuff that had taken days and weeks to make and silently swore revenge. A few years later I had great pleasure in refusing to supply her prestigious West End store.

But it was not all rejection. The *Daily Telegraph* wanted to feature the jewellery, but would only do so if there was a major supplier. Harvey Nichols in Knightsbridge was prepared to take some on sale or return but would only do so if backed by national newspaper coverage. Catch-22. So I rang both and told each that the other had agreed to go with it. Luckily they never contacted each other and we had our outlet and publicity.

And of the various fashion designers I cold-called, Bruce Oldfield was instantly generous and asked if we wanted to provide a range to accompany his next collection. It was a gamble, as we had to borrow money just to provide the samples, but we immediately realised that our jewellery would be worn by the most famous models and seen by the world's press. We decided to use chandelier drops that we had seen sold by an obscure Austrian firm called Swarovski. They couldn't believe that we intended to use these heavy – and very expensive – crystal drops, but we went ahead and started a craze for big paste jewellery. One of Sarah's designs was a chandelier drop with a hand-tied silk bow. It went on to become our trademark piece – we sold tens of thousands of pairs over the next few years, and it is now in the V & A's permanent collection.

Over the next five years we devoted our lives to the business. Once we got going it became successful very fast, with demand outstripping any possible supply. We could not afford to advertise, but we had a policy of making six pieces of every design that were solely for the use of the press. We would deliver anything free of charge to an editorial shoot anywhere in the world. In return, they had to get it all back to us in one piece or pay for it. The system worked – soon every magazine was full of Monty Don jewellery. We still have books of press cuttings that we can hardly bear to open. It seems long ago and far away.

Some pictures remain embarrassing every time you look at them…

All in a name

People understandably assumed that 'Monty Don' was just Montagu. His name alone was on everything we did together. However, it was still shocking the first time an important American buyer pushed past me, saying, 'Where is the STAR?' It was not surprising that I did not exist to her. She did not know who I was. But there he was, resplendent, head-to-toe in black and covered in jewels. (So was I, but clearly not so fetchingly as him.)

I would spend months working on a collection, drawing, refining, going backwards and forwards to the factory, checking samples, sorting out publicity. It was always a collaboration, though the factory owner who made up our jewellery only seemed to listen to Montagu. I was invisible. I was prepared to put up with this as long as the collection was made in time. Montagu's coming along and schmoozing him worked, but it was humiliating for me.

To be honest, I dreaded sticking my head above the parapet. I still like dwelling in the cosy bosom of my domestic life. If ever I have to do anything public I dread it. I wake in the middle of the night regretting that I have agreed to do it, longing to be struck by some illness that will excuse me from my fate. However, I loved the feeling of success when we got loads of press and the orders poured in.

The truth is that Montagu has always been noticed – not least by me. He is confident, photogenic, determined and a good designer in his own right. It was not surprising that he could charm the predominantly female buyers. But I also knew that he was acting. In his bones he was a writer, not a jeweller. He could sell so well because his soul was not invested in it. Whereas for me, this was the real thing. I also knew that the combination of the two of us, however it was divided up, invariably made a whole greater than the sum of our parts. He could – and can – annoy me more than anyone else I have ever met, but we do make a perfect team.

My birth certificate has me as 'George Montagu Don'. I had been named after my two grandfathers. The Montagu one – my mother's adored father – had died six months before I was born, but George Don – my father's tyrannical father – said that he did not wish his name to be associated with such an absurd name as Montagu. Stung perhaps by grief, my parents for once stood up to the old ogre and dropped George from the equation, adding in my father's name, Denis. When I was ten I rather unnecessarily added Wyatt, my mother's maiden name. So, by a circuitous route, I accumulated the name Montagu Denis Wyatt Don.

I was invariably known as Montagu, without any kind of abbreviation – especially not Monty, which my mother hated. Like a fool I must have told someone at school this, with the inevitable result that I was called Monty.

There was a sing-song, sneering tone to it. I assumed that it was not used in anything other than a hostile way.

I carried this assumption into adulthood, although more and more people would instinctively shorten my name to Monty without hostile intent. But my *real* name was Montagu and family and real friends still always called me that. Sarah has never, ever called me Monty.

But when we were looking round for a name for our new company a friend who worked in marketing said that we would be mad not to call it 'Monty Don'. He said that firms paid good money to invent names half as good. Everyone, he said, knew me as Monty. I was a real person and it was my name. Go with it.

So we did. This completely ignored the underlying basis of our partnership. We were equals in everything. To call the company after just one of us was insulting to the other and plain wrong. But the name was, as predicted, memorable and catchy. My signature became the logo and was trademarked around the world. Bags, boxes, shop signs, calling cards – all the paraphernalia of a business were emblazoned with it. But at home I was still always Montagu.

When I started writing I did so as Montagu, as much to liberate myself from the jewellery business as anything else. It was my real work so should therefore carry my real name. Later, when I was receiving counselling, the psychotherapist and I talked at length about the dualism of the names. I saw this as a terrible problem. If I was true to myself I should only call myself Montagu – yet almost everyone wanted to call me Monty. The wise man pointed out that this was only as much of a problem as I wanted it to be. I could easily be Montagu to Sarah and a handful of family and friends, and Monty to other people. Lots of writers and performers had *noms de plume*. Since then I have been easy about it. I now introduce myself as Monty; at home I am still Montagu. And my children call me Monty when they think I am getting above myself, which means that the public persona has intruded into the privacy of home.

The name 'Monty Don' became increasingly established. Once we got *Vogue*'s seal of approval everyone wanted to know. It sounds far-fetched now but one Fashion Week I remember seeing a line of limos outside our little mews workshop in Islington and it turned out that they were all press, TV crews or buyers from round the world queuing up to see us. Our timing – entirely accidental – was perfect. After the dreariness of the late Seventies and early Eighties people wanted glitz. It was the dawn of designer labels and fashion became glamorous; London was hot and we were in the centre of it. We found ourselves invited to 10 Downing Street, flying to New York and Paris and being fêted everywhere. I have an abiding image of Montagu striding through Manhattan, dressed as usual in black and covered in jewellery. We could always get a cab because he looked so amazing.

There were darker moments. We were robbed and lost all our orders, but somehow rode that storm. We had a protection racket operated on us by local gangsters and had to move workshop and showrooms overnight. This was genuinely scary. All the time we were expanding, and borrowing money hand over fist to finance it. Still, I look back upon it all as a glamorous time until the hurricane of October 1987. Thereafter it all went wrong.

The healer

It was constant work. We sold our jewellery across the world, with half going to America, opened our own shop in Beauchamp Place, Knightsbridge, designed collections for films, opera, theatre and various pop stars. We employed twenty-odd people and had hundreds of others making our stuff in various factories. We bought a house in Islington with a big garden, and the little spare time we had we spent in it. We had our first child Adam. We enjoyed our work, were filled with love for him and for each other. But I was deeply unhappy. There was a discontent that travelled around with me. I felt chronically, but vaguely, unwell. My temper veered from the irascible to the unreasonable. This, as I hit my early thirties, was the way life was. I had a wife I loved and who loved me well, one adored child and another on the way, a business that seemed to be romping from success to success, a clothes rail filled with black and baggy designer clothes, a house fixed up as we wanted it with a garden out the back that I loved and was proud of, and yet I was angry with my own skin. Nothing suited.

I went to see a healer. I can't remember if he was a herbalist, acupuncturist, homeopath or white-coated faith healer, but I liked him. He had tried to blow his head off with a shotgun, failed, and whilst they were putting his face back together he decided to reassemble his life in a different order. After spending some years in China studying traditional medicine he had set up a small surgery. I would go there once a week to be dosed with vile-tasting brown concoctions. ('How do you feel this week?' *Much worse.* 'Great! That means the toxins are coming out.') He had me abstain from tea, coffee and alcohol, and described my various symptoms with unerring accuracy.

But after a few months of this puritanical regime he told me that I was unhealable. His medicines, for all the efficacy with which they squeezed the toxicity from me, were a waste of his time at the pestle and mortar. In his judgement, there was only one right course of action, which was to give up work immediately and spend at least a year working on the land.

Just for a fleeting moment the idea held a shred of delicious practicality. He was offering not so much a cure as a reprieve. Then reality barged back in. It was absurd. I had wife, child, employees, and orders to deliver. So he discharged me. He could do no more. We never saw each other again.

He was, however, spot on. I needed the land and always had done. I have gardened since I was a small boy because, along with my four brothers and sisters, I was press-ganged into work in the garden from a very early age. For about ten years I served something between an apprenticeship and a period of slavery, mowing lawns, weeding paths, picking and thinning vegetables and constantly hoeing.

But when I was 17, I had an epiphany of sorts. I was sowing carrot seeds on a mild, midgy evening after school. I had prepared the chalky loam into a fine tilth so that the hoe ran an easy drill along the line of string marking the row. The soil was warm and drying on my fingers. I took pinches of the seed from the other cupped palm and tried to sow it as thinly as possible, knowing that any extra time and trouble taken at this stage was more than saved when it came to thinning the emerging seedlings later. The less thinning the better, as it attracted carrot fly. I did and knew these things without thinking. But I suddenly realised that I was completely content. This was what I liked doing.

A few days later I had a dream in which my fingers worked down into that same soil and grew down into the ground. I woke very happy. To this day I get the same sense of well-being from working my hands into loose soil as some people get from smelling the sea or the buzz of a football crowd. It is that feeling of being in the right place at the right time. So, from seeing gardening as a variety of household drudgery, it became – overnight – something that I have always loved every minute of. This is an acceptable enthusiasm when you reach a certain age, but was odd then and, to preserve any fragments of street cred, I kept quiet about it.

By the time I was an adult I had come to need regular contact with the soil. I still do. If I go for a few days without gardening – not telly-gardening but proper everyday digging, planting or weeding – I become restless and dissatisfied.

Plastic tulips

As a child I was allowed to run wild in the woods and fields surrounding the Cambridgeshire village I grew up in. There were lots of children of the same age and we all built camps, had gangs. We knew the time by the chiming of the church clock and I knew every wood and hedgerow round the village.

My favourite place was a spinney that was full of primroses at Easter and bluebells in May.

I lived with my parents in a little gate lodge at the bottom of a winding drive to a magical Georgian rectory with an overgrown, rampant garden. Our garden, and my aunt and uncle's next door, were neat and tidy and had tea roses with names like 'Superstar' and 'Peace'. There seemed to be a lot of bare earth around them. I used to hide behind the hollyhocks when powdery relations came to visit as I loathed being kissed by them.

I made my first garden from a technicolour display of plastic flowers I bought with my pocket money. On a Saturday we could get a lift into town all crammed on the back seat of Uncle Ted's Rover. Woolworths was a treasure trove, with a huge plastic flower section upstairs – I bought great sprays of lily of the valley, gaudy daffodils with stiff plastic leaves. To add to my collection I was given the red plastic tulips that came free with packets of Daz from the village shop. My friend Ann and I ringed our tree house with edging stones painted bright blue and pushed the fake flowers into the ground surrounding them. It always looked dazzling.

I didn't have another garden until my twenties, when I had a little house in Cambridge with a back yard 15 feet by 25 feet. I didn't know where to start. I had never dug over a garden, knew nothing about soil and even less about what to plant in it. The first thing I did was to place a few herbaceous plants that I had been given tight up to the low wall that edged the garden. This is a fault that almost everyone makes – planting close to a wall will mean poor dry soil, resulting in unhappy plants. So many back gardens follow the pattern of narrow borders round the edge with a bit of tatty lawn in the middle. Mine was no different. I was clueless.

I always loved the walled Fellows' Gardens in Cambridge. Not only because of trysts I had in them as a schoolgirl, but I recognised them as beautiful gardens, even if I didn't understand why. They were secret places you could slip into – each one was the essence of a garden, a *hortus conclusus*, an enclosure where nature was controlled and tamed.

I realise now that the fenland landscape of Cambridge is very similar to this particular part of Herefordshire where we now live. There is the same constant wind, although thankfully ours comes mainly from the west, whereas in Cambridge a biting easterly blew in from the Urals. On gloomy days it can seem unrelentingly flat and characterless, but when the sun shines I love the sense of expansiveness. It becomes a silvery lake in flood and a lush water meadow in summer.

Gardening together

When Sarah and I looked for a house in London, we wanted as big a garden as possible. This turned out to be in De Beauvoir, an unfashionable area right on the Islington/Hackney border, just a mile from the centre of the City. It was an end-of-terrace house that had annexed next door's garden after the house attached to it had been bombed in the war. Two gardens for the price of one. It was irresistible.

From the first, Sarah and I gardened together. When I was wooing her I said that I could help her in her new garden in Cambridge. The result was that I ended up cutting her tatty lawn with a pair of scissors. High horticulture. But it started a genuine partnership in the garden that has endured.

Every aspect of design, each remotely significant bit of planting has been discussed and shared over the past 25 years. I cannot separate my adult experience of gardening from this. I do most of the heavy work, and I don't think she has ever touched any kind of grass-cutting implement, but there are no demarcation lines. We work as absolute equals. Some of our happiest times together have been when we have both been working outside, doing different jobs in different parts of the garden, hardly speaking but bound by a common purpose.

Whilst our peer group were gadding about the clubs of Eighties London, we made our garden. We worked hugely long hours building the business, but Sundays were always spent in the garden; in summer I was out there until it was too dark to see and often up again at five to do more until I left for work. We poured ourselves into it.

But by 1987 the garden was made. I am not by nature a primper and preener and although it was good and could absorb as much time as I had spare to give it, it did not satisfy my desire for space. I wanted landscape around me and I wanted my own piece of it to make into a private space. I always come back to this visceral need to scrape a hollow in the ground. It has to do with the literal earth. The herbalist knew me better than I knew myself – earth heals me better than any medicine.

Early days in our Hackney garden, about 1983.

Moving on

I jumped ship. Not that anyone would have noticed. I didn't tell anyone, least of all myself. But I gave up my allegiance to the business and London, including the garden. I still did all the things that were expected of me, but I only gave as much as would sustain the impression of being wholehearted. This was a hopeless state of affairs. It has to be all or nothing, and nothing is never enough. Anyway, a small business is like a marriage – you cannot just walk out on it without tearing the whole thing apart, but I thought that perhaps I could just slip away without anyone really noticing. I should have had the guts to make a clean break. Instead I was storing up trouble for the future.

When we were in business the whole set-up felt wrong. Even though we were completely involved in every aspect of running the company it always seemed like an uncomfortable shoe, pinching and painful. I hated the routine of having to be in early, before anyone else, and of staying after everyone had left. Often my assistant was sent off to museums to find inspiration for some new project while I drew the short straw and was stuck in the office, chained down by Montagu's puritan work ethic, dulled by duty.

October 1987 was a turning point. A great storm ripped the southern part of the country apart, flattening our garden in the process. A few days later the stock market crashed. This affected America more than Europe; half our US orders were cancelled, reducing our annual turnover by a quarter. Our own shop sales fell. At the same time interest rates started to rise uncontrollably and our shop and office rents more than doubled. With hindsight we should have extricated ourselves there and then, but at the time we assumed that, like everything else, we could take it in our stride.

Our daughter Freya was born at the end of 1987 and I was determined that the two children should be brought up in the country as I had been. I wanted them to grow up with fields around them. The home counties were too expensive and too near. I needed to be far away from London. We looked as far afield as Cornwall but eventually bought a large house with 35 acres in Herefordshire. This was the very peak of the late Eighties property boom, when you could exchange a small terraced house in London for a country estate.

One small hitch was that we had not yet sold our London house. But at that time house prices were increasing weekly. The asking price named was invariably just the starting point for any bid. So we blithely took out a bridging loan, confident that not only would we sell our London house within a few weeks, but for a higher price. It seemed then that prices would keep on rising and that any delay in selling would only ensure a higher figure when eventually you did sell. But all bubbles burst, and this one was at popping point.

I was ill for months after our daughter was born despite having had a supposedly film-star birth at an enormously expensive private London hospital. As soon as my five-day package was up I was discharged. However, I had a slipped disc, a result of the bodged delivery, and was so anaemic that I needed a blood transfusion. My injuries were not acknowledged and as we tried to leave the hospital I had to walk down three flights of stairs because the lift had broken. They made us pay our bill there and then. It was a purely financial transaction – just like a hotel – and they couldn't have cared less about the state that I was in. I was unable to walk or stand properly for over a year.

But the business had to be kept going. As I lay in bed recuperating Montagu dangled a sketchbook over me and I drew the next collection. Neither of us could cope.

House prices spiralled down almost from the day we moved to Herefordshire. Interest rates started to rise. Mrs Thatcher's chickens were coming home to roost. We finally sold our house in Ufton Road a year later having run up £30,000 in interest on the bridging loan.

The Hanburies

I have written about our two and a half years at The Hanburies in *The Prickotty Bush*. It is the story of an obsession, a broken heart, a broken spirit, a broken business but not, thank God, a broken marriage.

From the moment that we first visited the place in April 1988, I became consumed with the desire to transform the land around the house into a garden. I schemed, dreamed and planned constantly and, once we moved in, gave

The big white house on a Herefordshire hillside. It was our domain and we loved every blade of grass of it.

literally every spare moment to the project. I was 33 and in my prime. I felt fit and strong and had almost boundless energy. It was as though all the frustration of the London years was released on to this Herefordshire hillside.

I loved it there. From the first I knew that I could happily spend the rest of my life there and, ideally, be buried on the hillside. This instant infatuation did not seem odd. I had had exactly the same sensation when I first met Sarah, despite her being married to someone else. I knew that she was the one. It took a little time and a divorce to sort things out but I was right.

The place had little other than space to commend it. My response was entirely based on instinct. The garden had been used for many years to graze up to thirty horses at a time, effectively vandalising it. But it was indescribably beautiful, set on a steep hillside looking over the Frome valley and across to the Black Mountains. A long drive flanked by a line of huge wellingtonias took you halfway up the hill to the house. Two-thirds of our land was made up of fields too steep to cultivate. Orchids flowered at the top of the hill in June. Below the house it was wet and heavy with grass as lush as buttered asparagus.

When we arrived the docks were head high, brambles yards deep and elder sprouting everywhere. The first year I spent most of my time cutting things back. There was a five-acre mature orchard and next to that a two-acre wood where buzzards nested and foxes had an earth. We cleared much of the fallen timber and brambles and the following year thousands of primroses flowered under the trees. Along one edge of the wood was a ditch, which became a stream that ran into a clogged-up medieval fishpond. I unclogged it all and discovered a Victorian rockery. Now exposed, the mud started to sprout skunk cabbage, gunnera, peltiphyllum, rheum and irises.

I dug the old kitchen garden, adding the only good thing that in my book ever comes from horses – mountains of muck. We put up a greenhouse and some cold frames and within a year were pretty much self-sufficient in vegetables. I made three terraces where there had been a steep slope, moving

hundreds of tons of rock and soil from one side of the house to the other.
My favourite place to go if I needed to rest or hide was the orchard, where
the owls also hid in the sprawling, unpruned apple trees during the day, their
astonishing purple eyes watching from the branches. I would scramble up the
steep bank with the dogs and sit under a tree, seeing everything in the valley
and knowing that no one could see me. Then, when I was ready, I could go back
down the hill to face the world again.

Although Montagu was always outside and seemed to have a clear vision
of what he was trying to achieve, the scale of the place was overwhelming.
I would wander down to find him, but everything seemed so far away.
The children were tiny and we had terrible nights, and the business
was very demanding. It was a happy time but exhausting. I put any spare
energy and time that I had into making the house habitable.

Early morning, August 1988, looking down on the Frome valley from the orchard. The best days of my life.

Garden diary

Throughout this period I kept a diary. It wasn't an easy time.

28th June 1989. Today would have been my father's 74th birthday. I recognise his awkward brand of fear in the way that I can only cope with our money pressures by hiding in the garden under the cover of hard physical labour. Last night Sarah said, 'You've got a streak of craziness that is endlessly tiring.'

It is true. It is my father's inheritance and is in no way a virtue. Sarah longs for a good, kind man who will be a rock to build herself on. But I am always too tired to be kind, too weary to give anything at all.

8th July 1989. My birthday. I came downstairs to the strains of 'Happy Birthday' played on the tambourine and sung with great gusto by Adam. On the table was a line of pots, a Ceanothus *'Burkwoodii', a* Lonicera periclymenum *'Graham Thomas', a true Virginia creeper and a fig. These were carefully chosen by Sarah, each plant for an exact spot. They are the best of presents. To be greeted like this by my two children, my beautiful and loving wife, my dogs I adore, the weather clearing by the minute outside the window, should have been the best of all possible happinesses.*

I was miserable all day.

How can I plant these things, when their future will not be our future? The new owners will pull them down or ignore them. I have to shake this off, or else all hope is lost, all spirit defeated by bankers and accountants. Live for the day. Garden for your children.

9th July 1989. This morning Sarah told me that I wasn't married to her any more, I was married to the garden. I think that I am flattered by this.

14th July 1989. The major criticism always put to me about this garden is that it is so harsh and inhospitable – to which I immediately counter that the most homely house was once a building site. But there is some truth in the criticism. I don't look for comfort or ease in a garden. It is a reflection of me and is correspondingly bleak.

7th August 1989. Last night Sarah came out with one of her periodic pronouncements about the design of the place, to the effect that much was wrong as opposed to incomplete. I have learned to listen to these amazingly annoying suggestions because she has always thought long and hard about them and is nearly always correct. I blunder and bluster into chance success; she slowly finds it and isolates it.

Escape

I made a herb garden, a cutting garden, walks flanked by pleached hornbeams and limes, perennial borders, a large lawn, planted trees and hedges, and worked as hard as I think anyone could have done – hardly slept, outside all day in all weather, writing at night with clumsy fingers, not daring to open letters or

The Hanburies potting shed was often more cosy than the house.

answer the phone because all roads led to bankruptcy and defeat. In winter I worked under lights in the dark and in summer worked until my energy ran out. Often I would be too tired to walk back to the house and have to make my way back in stages. I gave the place more than I had, used up reserves that will never be replenished, and it was all utter folly because every day – every hour – we were running up these ruinous debts.

> While Montagu was madly making the garden I went into hospital for tests on my back, and the side effect was chemical meningitis brought on by a reaction to the myelogram. Having walked in, I was carried out and spent two bedridden weeks vomiting in a dark room.
>
> It seemed a constant battle to get well enough to deal with the daily demands of little children and a manic husband. We both dreaded the post. It never seemed to bring anything good. Just solicitors' letters, bills and problems. Even now, fifteen years later, Montagu can scarcely bring himself to open a letter. I will never know if the strain of trying to sort out the mess made me ill, or whether it was a long controlled breakdown that occasionally manifested itself in a complete physical collapse.

Shut up and get on with it

My mother, still in her sixties, had a heart attack and died around this time. I suspect that she was both proud and bewildered by my involvement with jewellery, although she never wore any of it. She hated travelling and never visited me in any of my homes. This meant that she never saw a garden I made, never read a word I published, and never saw me on television. She was not good at showing affection. But there was love, albeit understood rather than displayed, and if she was hard on her five children, she was even harder on herself. She was an intensely anxious, driven woman, equally intolerant of failure or success unless it was accompanied by visible effort. If you felt unwell, she would snap 'Are you ill?'; if you said yes, you were told to go to bed. If you did not go to bed, you were therefore not ill and should shut up and get on with it. Her worst condemnation was to call you idle. I, of course, with my head nearly always in a book, was often idle. In many ways I do not regret her regime. It made all us children into hard workers, expecting nothing of life that we were not prepared to do or make ourselves.

I had invited her to see our new home, wanting to impress her with the scale of the undertaking. She was planning to make her visit in the summer, but she died in April. My father had died six years earlier and now parentless, her death left me relieved, saddened and confused.

Fame, if not fortune

It is funny how some ideas, seemingly very simple, catch the imagination. The move from the city to the country was still a novel idea then, and I was commissioned to write a book about the first year of making the garden. This became *The Prickotty Bush*. The *Mail on Sunday*, for whom I had written a couple of articles, also hired me to write a monthly report on my progress. Other papers and magazines began to accept articles from me. Almost by accident, I was at last becoming a writer.

Writing led to television. A researcher saw one of the *Mail on Sunday* pieces and caught me on one of the rare occasions that I answered the phone. He said they were looking for a younger, unknown gardening presenter. Would I do a screen test? I had never heard of the programme – I'm not sure I knew then that there was such a thing as daytime telly – but I said I would, did, and a few weeks later found myself broadcasting live from a makeshift garden in the car park outside the studios in Liverpool's Albert Dock. I was unafraid because I had no idea what I was doing. I simply spoke to the camera imagining that I was talking to Sarah's aunt in Leominster.

After four or five weekly stints I was summonsed to Granada's head office in Manchester. Assuming that my amateurish bluff had been called, I went with a heavy heart. However, instead of being sacked I was asked if I wanted to make 26 ten-minute gardening films, one a week. We would start next Tuesday. I found out later that *This Morning* had been told to come up with a gardening strand at short notice. I just happened to be the person in place at the time.

For the next six months, on top of frantically trying to shore up the business, writing articles, writing my first book and gardening every moment I could, each week I would travel to a garden in some corner of Britain. There I would meet the director, a man 25 years older than me with a lifetime of experience in television. He and I would then recce the location carefully. We would work out the angles of the sun, and all the logistical practicalities of filming. Then we would sit down with a cup of tea or a pint of beer and he would not let me leave the room until we had worked out the entire film, with words, locations, camera angles, cutaways, all in fifteen-second segments. It was a bit prescriptive but proved to be extremely useful training. Along with the regular live work in the studio in Liverpool, I was receiving a crash course in all kinds of television presenting. But for many years I assumed that the work would disappear as suddenly as it came. However, whilst it lasted the money was vital.

Vital in that it slowed the rate of decline, but not enough to influence the outcome. The overdraft sank deeper and deeper, and interest rates doubled within twelve months. A bad situation got worse every day. The banks wanted their money and started to bounce our cheques whilst simultaneously adding their charges – and interest on them – to the tally.

Collapse

Of course it could not go on. Something had to give. As it turned out, that something proved to be our shop, our business, our savings, our furniture – and our home. We had the choice of being declared bankrupt or selling up what we had, paying back what we owed and starting again. The latter seemed the only honourable course of action. This took time and turned out to be tricky because the value of our assets was falling weekly. And still we were trading as normal, trying to appear as positive as possible to encourage sales. Walking away would have been far easier.

I rang a well-known designer and asked his advice. 'Flush it down the toilet', was his immediate reply. 'Everybody will hate you for a week and then forget all about it.' But we could not bring ourselves to do that, although with hindsight it would have been much cleaner and less painful. We were nice middle-class people brought up to do the right thing.

We had an outstanding debt of £35,000 with one of our manufacturers. For nine months we sweated blood to repay him bit by bit. Finally, after many sleepless nights, we had to admit that we couldn't raise the last £3,000. We went for a walk in Kew Gardens to tell him, knowing this would be ammunition enough to make us bankrupt. But all he said was, 'That's okay. I knew you couldn't pay it.' My gut response was not gratitude or relief but fury. I wanted to hit him. He seemed so dismissive of something that had blighted us for months. But it was another lesson. It would have been far better to have told him about it long before things reached this pass.

11th October 1989. Today a young man from a Hereford estate agent called to take instructions on the sale of the house. He reckons that we will be lucky to get what we paid for it. Sarah and I stumble through these days, seeing things drift through our fingers, wasting time and yet without motive to do anything about it.

Titanic

When I completed *The Prickotty Bush* at the beginning of 1990, the house was still on the market. Buyers came and went. Some found it too shabby, others too daunting, and it remained unsold for another whole year, which was a strangely happy time.

2nd September 1990. George told me that the other day when driving along he saw a peacock land on a power line. For a moment it swung heavily, then suddenly exploded before his eyes – a wonder followed by horror. It had touched two lines and the electricity fried it.

I finished making flights of fancy steps from the top terrace to the rose terrace and from there down on to the lawn, using the oak fencing posts that we took down two years ago. To hold them in place I used hazel pegs, which had to be cut from the wood, sawn into lengths, split and then sharpened.

The pair of young owls have spent the last month living in the orchard by day and kicking up an appalling racket at night. One screeches and the other instantly replies. They are very tame. I have shone my torch into their faces a number of times. They are vividly coloured, all bright russets and ochres, each feather lapping colour on colour.

I gardened blithely on, still trying to be true to the vision. I wanted to finish what I had started and tried to squeeze as much as possible into every extra day there. During that year Sarah became pregnant again and in December our youngest son, Tom, was born in a blizzard. The snow remained thick well into the spring and we tobogganed down the hillside. I have photographs of us with the exhilarated smiles shared by dancers on the *Titanic*.

The shop was eventually sold for approximately one-tenth of what it had cost. We could not even give away the fixtures and fittings – which had cost a fortune. In the end we found a buyer for the house who seemed to genuinely

care for the place. The process of selling it was utterly prosaic. The rituals were enacted, paper was exchanged and we no longer had anything to do with it.

The Victorian rockery, which had been completely submerged in mud and brambles.

When it came down to it, Montagu was a loony and I was ill all the time. How did we ever believe that we could have saved the situation?

I suppose the lowest point for me was when I was hidden away on my sickbed while potential buyers traipsed round the house. I found it astonishing that Montagu never mentioned my bedridden weeks in *The Prickotty Bush*. I can only assume that he was so obsessed with making the garden that I was, during that time, peripheral.

Despite everything, Montagu had the garden and a book. I am sad that I have so little to show for that time. At least the children were happy and healthy.

Homeless

We moved out of the big house over the course of a week, saving money on removals by hiring a van and doing it ourselves, sliding up and down the long drive in the snow. Sarah's mother let us have a spare bedroom in their house and I spent the last night in The Hanburies alone, with no furniture, sleeping on the floor of the sitting room by a fire. I felt driven out, a refugee. I don't want to over-egg the pudding. We survived. No one died. But for the record, the worst thing was not the loss of creature comforts but the humiliation. I felt a complete and utter fool.

It was not just me, of course. Sarah drove down the drive on 15th February 1991, her 37th birthday, with three children under five, also having simultaneously lost her job, her business and her home. But she, unlike me, did not lapse into self-fixated depression. She got on with it. The one thing of which both of us were sure was that we would never go back into the jewellery business. By then there were no good memories.

> I now look back upon the sale of The Hanburies as a positive thing, cutting free from its bourgeois decorations and the need to create a sense of family history with inherited furniture and paintings. Is this what psychiatrists call a 'sense of entitlement'? By getting rid of our stuffy furniture and velvet curtains, third-rate watercolours and knick-knacks, we were free to start again. The Eighties were the last gasp of aspiration to aristocratic living, with all the dreadful pretensions that this involved. We were not guiltless. But increasingly I felt uncomfortable pretending to be anything other than ourselves. It was a liberation to have left it all behind.

Charting the rise and fall

Just as television had fallen easily into my lap, a couple of months after we moved I found out how fickle a mistress it could be. Although I was still under contract to Granada, they decided that it would be cheaper to pay me to stay at home and repeat my old films than make new ones. Being paid to stay at home seemed pretty good for the first few weeks, but it could not hide the fact that I was not being offered any new work. It was then followed by months of appearing regularly on television, seemingly gainfully and glamorously employed, whereas in reality I had no work at all. There was a complete collapse of all media activity at the beginning of the Nineties; any scraps of freelance work paid at literally half the rates that had been offered twelve months earlier.

At the beginning of 1992 *Harpers & Queen* rang up and asked if I would like to do an article about our experiences in the Eighties. They explained that they were looking for a piece that would illustrate the shifting fortunes at the fag end of Thatcherism. I agreed, thinking that I would enjoy writing it and enjoy getting paid for it even more. Arrangements were made for a photographer to come and then, a phone call later, for 'the writer to visit'. I was too embarrassed and feeble to query this, even though the only reason for doing it had been to earn some money. So one very cold and foggy January day we found ourselves being interviewed by Neil Lyndon. He was an extremely nice man and wrote an excellent, accurate piece. But his seven-page feature carried the heading 'Monty Don went from boom to bust in a decade. Neil Lyndon charts the rise and fall of a glittering empire'. Just a year or so earlier *Harpers* had been one of our main editorial outlets. All in all it was a pretty pointless exercise, celebrating failure when all we had wanted was to earn some money by writing an article.

Nobody loves you when you're down and out

Throughout 1991 and 1992 I had no more than a dozen days' work and for all of 1992 I was on the dole. The unemployment agency would give you a travel pass if you showed them an invitation to a formal job interview. But the media does not work like that. To get work in newspapers or television you have to put yourself about. It is vital to pop in to offices and see people – however tenuous the contact. Being in the right place at the right time is as much a matter of judgement and manipulation as luck. But all my contacts were in London, Manchester or Liverpool. We had around £120 per week to cover everything. The cheapest train ticket to London was around £40. The journey, then as now, was all but four hours each way. Bus and tube fares might add another £5. I simply could not afford to network on the off chance of work – even though I knew that it was my only chance of making things happen.

I remember visiting a production company in Clerkenwell, having had a phone call gushing about the stuff they had seen me do on television. When I was 'next in town' I 'dropped in' to see them. For an hour they picked my brains about a series that duly appeared about a year later – without me, but with all my suggestions. I left them with only a pound coin in my pocket. So I set off walking back to Paddington, wondering whether to invest it in a cup of tea or a bus ride. On the way I walked past the offices of a very well-known fashion designer who we had known for years. We had done collections together, been on holiday together, often dined in each other's homes. We had had little contact over the previous year, but even so I dropped in. The reception was distinctly chilly. Although it was lunchtime, no mention of food or drink was made, let alone offered. I brazened it out for twenty minutes, behaving as though we were experiencing a spot of turbulence but no more than a blip in generally tricky times, but it was apparent that I was *persona non grata*. I must have reeked of failure. I left hungry and dispirited and angry – not least with myself for wallowing in self-pity and bitterness.

However, my mother, in death, came to the rescue. Her will was eventually sorted out and she left me some stocks and shares. I sold these the very same hour – the only shares I have ever owned – and they raised enough money for the deposit on a house.

House hunting

We visited 68 different houses that summer and autumn. Of these there were only three that we wanted to live in. We were outbid at auction on two of them, and pulled out on the third when we found that there was a plan to build a bypass at the foot of the garden. Finally we heard about our current house, which had been abandoned by its owner, who had bought it a year earlier, pulled it to pieces, but never moved in before fleeing the country and his debts.

We bumped down the sunken lane to the old farmhouse and felt a lurch of excitement, went through the door and knew we wanted it. As it was a repossession it was going absurdly cheaply. Admittedly it lacked water, electricity, sanitation, any interior walls and, as it turned out, had a roof that was about to slide off, but it felt right. We managed somehow to rustle up a mortgage even though we had no real income – and persuaded a wealthy friend to buy a stake in it. Eventually we took proud possession of a building heavy with history but officially unfit for human habitation.

We had a survey done by a historic buildings expert, who dated the house by the mouldings on the carved beams and found the gable ends of a medieval hall hidden within the derelict shell. This would affect every decision we made as to how to repair the fabric without inflicting further damage.

We couldn't live in it until the basic services were installed. It had never had running water nor electricity. Our predecessor had begun to try to modernise it, but given up. He had gutted the house, stripping out walls and floors, removing all the Victorian lath and plaster, and revealing the skeleton of a timber-framed Tudor building.

We had taken on a cold, damp ruin, but the rooms were high-ceilinged and there would be plenty of space. It was far bigger than anything else we had looked at.

Our new home, a timber-framed farmhouse with a dilapidated hopkiln that we bought a few years later.

It came with nearly two acres of overgrown rough land and this meant we could start a garden from scratch. All that existed was an ancient hazel and a scraggy hawthorn on the edge of a ditch. I realise it is very rare to begin something without having any existing features other than the layout of the buildings and a wall. It was a new beginning.

The garden was laid out in all its three-dimensional glory in Montagu's mind long before anything actually happened. He could visualise every detail and spent hours of every day drawing and thinking about it. I find the certainty of this kind of vision extraordinary as well as his ability to completely ignore what is going on all around him. I was in a blur of childcare, and looking back there are great blanks from which I remember nothing. It was all I could do to keep the children happy, warm and fed, and try to live in the present, despite the constant worry of our finances.

We both became obsessed with the provenance and structure of the building. Montagu spent days in the county records library and we kept extensive records of every tiny detail of the building. I immersed myself in restoration techniques, and we both went on a course for lime plastering, and visited as many buildings of the same period as we possibly could. We knew straight away that it was a plum of a building.

The house was repaired as it had been built 500 years previously, with lime mortar, lime wash and oak. No plasterboard or cement was allowed, unless there was no alternative. This takes much longer than modern techniques but it means that the building has not lost its Tudor atmosphere. Our lack of capital proved to be an advantage because everything had to happen more slowly and more thoughtfully than if a stack of money had been thrown at it.

Rock bottom

So, having spent eight months lodging with Sarah's parents, we rented a farmhouse a mile or so down the road from our new house. This place may have looked charming from the outside, but was damp, cold and rat-infested.

In the kitchen only the fridge was a rat-free zone. We would hear them scrabbling in the cutlery drawers in the evening whilst we ate and watch them hopping on the lawn in broad daylight. We set traps and if the snared creature wasn't disposed of immediately it was invariably half-eaten within hours. For three months Tom slept with us because we were frightened they would attack him in his cot. It was a symptom of our apathy that we never thought of asking the landlord to do something about this.

When you have no money things that you have taken for granted become a major obstacle. One of these was simply getting around. Our nearest shop was five miles away, the children's village school two miles. There was no public transport. Just getting them to and from school took petrol and wear and tear. We dreaded the roadside hedges being cut because it usually resulted in a puncture that cost a third of our weekly income to repair. Buying shoes for the children was a constant problem. Everything was a constant problem. There were often times when Sarah and I would make bread and jam our main meal so that the children could eat well.

The whole experience of being unemployed is generally punitive. Your spirit sinks to the same level as your standard of living. I learned to despise anyone who belittles the unemployed by accusing them of being workshy or lazy.

Irritated, unreasonable, unwell and impossible, I sank into deeper depression. I began to believe that I would never work again.

This was the lowest point. Sarah told me that she could not cope with me any longer. If I saw a doctor she would stand by me. If I refused she would go. So I went and saw my GP about my various physical symptoms and then, rather ashamed, admitted that I 'felt a little low'.

Chemical ease

Pills eased me. I will never forget the bliss of standing at the kitchen sink in that horrid farmhouse, doing the washing up and realising, about ten days after starting a course of Prozac, that rinsing this cup, drying that plate was wholly satisfying. I was without anger or regret. Through the window the thin February sun fell on the matted grass and the buds of a winter jasmine. No sunset has ever been more beautiful. It was, despite the surroundings, heaven.

For about a month I felt as though I was on holiday in a seaside town, pottering about, unhurried, enjoying the day. This evolved into a less ecstatic, more prosaic frame of mind that enabled me to face the world and made me slightly easier to live with. If the drugs took my emotions off the roller coaster and gently bedded them down, a course of cognitive therapy gave my brain the tools to react and change. I spent months carving large wooden bowls from blocks of wood from trees blown down in our garden in the great storm of January 1990. Whilst I was aware that this counted as little more than therapy, I was content.

Depression: a user's guide

What is it like to be depressed? The truth is that when you are depressed the last thing you are going to do is sit down and describe it. And when you are not depressed to some extent you forget and to some extent you deliberately try to avoid remembering. There is nothing good in it. Nothing to be gained.

Light levels affect me greatly. My two worst times of year are invariably the ten weeks leading up to the winter solstice on 21st December, and early July following the summer solstice of 21st June. In winter I now use light boxes, which help enormously. I also take a great deal of exercise. Gardening combines all the beneficial qualities of sunlight, weather, activity and a sense of purpose. It is the ideal activity to heal mind hurt. In winter I exercise more systematically, five days a week for an hour or so on top of any gardening that I do. This obviously does my body no harm – but much more significantly, it does my mind a great deal of good.

There are phases of decline. The first intimation is the sense of something else there, almost in another dimension. It is like looking at a galaxy in the night sky with your naked eye: if you look directly it is invisible, but as you turn your head away you catch a flicker of it in the corner of your eye. Nevertheless, you can feel happy and good. But every now and then horror or sorrow push forward. It can be controlled. But it is there.

The next stage is that this 'normal' world feels as though it is resting on thin ice that hides unimaginable depths. The trick is to keep going forward, don't look down and don't lose your nerve. But this is tiring and when you get tired the momentum becomes much harder to sustain. The look on someone's face as you pass in the car breaks your heart. Sometimes it can be inanimate objects. I have been reduced to tears by leaves blowing under the car. You are sane enough to know that this is odd and stupid and completely irrational. But not sane enough to avoid a great emotional tearing. This, of course, is unseen, unspoken, unshared. You are fine and you have every reason to be. Life is rich.

Often this stage can be reversed. Nothing works better than a day in the garden, doing simple jobs, listening to the radio, cooking a meal.

But it can then lead to a much more prosaic stage where you feel grumpy and nothing pleases. Everything irritates. You are awkward in your own skin. You are always left waiting too long, or constantly rushed. Everything you come across has a sharp, abrasive edge. People speak too slowly or too fast, too quietly or too loud. In fact a pretty consistent symptom is an increased sensitivity to noise. You find yourself shouting at a child to be quiet because they asked a simple question or sang.

Above all, it is exhausting. Everything is an effort. Really everything. Not doing anything does not bring any relief. In fact I have found that the more physical exercise I make myself take, the more energy is fed back into the system. But it doesn't store long. The next day I start from scratch again. Some days it is all I can do to lift my head off my chest. My skull feels as heavy as a boulder.

I hardly sleep. There is a blessed two or three hours of oblivion when I go to sleep before waking at 1 or 2 am and tossing and turning till 5, when I often give up sleep as a bad job. That first half hour out of bed is usually the best time of the day. As the kettle boils I resolve to clear the backlog, clear a space. I never do. Just fail again.

I do not do any of the things that matter, any of the things that would help. Letters, emails, phone calls remain unanswered. Plants are not planted, harvests not gathered, work is not delivered. Nothing is tidied or put away. I wear the same clothes every day. I eat too much yet cannot be bothered to cook or shop properly. Concentration for more than five minutes at a time is practically impossible. Everything slides away.

Triggers

When I am going down I become extremely susceptible to images or music.
A snatch of song heard on a tinny radio through an open window or a picture
caught flicking through a newspaper will tumble me into despair. Opening the
paper one day I saw a black and white picture from the Second World War of a
young Serb being held down by a group of laughing Croat soldiers, all smiling
for the camera, with guns, knives and a two-handed saw in position ready to
remove his head. For days this horror tormented me, stopped me sleeping or
eating. Some days later I followed a council machine cutting the verges. It was
the second week in May and the cow parsley was at its best, lining the roads
with its foaming flower. Cow parsley is one of the great glories of the British
countryside. To smash it down whilst it is in flower is always philistine and
unnecessary but on that day it seemed to me an act of unspeakable horror,
collating wartime barbarism with bureaucratic vandalism, and I found myself
and the car in a ditch, hysterical.

Petty illness accompanies all of this. The body becomes a burden.
Your immune system packs up. Your bowels go haywire, your teeth ache.
Your hair falls out and your skin erupts, cracks or sags. Sarah always says that
I turn a yellowish grey when I am very down. It is all physical, all painful,
uncomfortable and often disgusting. The body seems to be saying, don't you
believe me? *I'm ill.* I remember one particularly grim November week I had
dysentery, a bad sinus infection and thrush simultaneously. Happy days.

All my senses become overloaded. My head crowds with unwanted
sounds, images and memories. Sometimes I wish there was a pill or injection
that would send me into a dreamless sleep for a week. I remember one summer's
weekend staying with friends and knowing that I was tumbling faster than I
could hide. I realised that the only way I could cope at all was to go and lie in the
white-walled guest bedroom. But although the room was minimally furnished a
small painting on one wall made it impossible to rest. It was as intolerable to my

eye as a heavy blanket on a feverish patient. Yet I felt immobilised on the bed, unable to get up and take it down. Outside the window the sky was clear blue and the children were laughing and playing in a paddling pool. For a while their laughter was a torment. And then there was sleep.

When I'm ill, there is nothing much that I can do about it. I cannot work or garden. I feed the hens and open the greenhouses and go to bed. But nowadays this stage does not last long. After about a week I know that I have to fight it. It is not a case of 'pulling my socks up' or 'getting a grip' or any of the other pointless platitudes. It is a quieter, grimmer struggle. I battle it. It becomes a straight contest between me and it, and often I am left down and broken, but I have learned not to give in. This struggle is entirely physical. I will concentrate on holding my head up for minutes at a time. This can be exhausting and pointless but it helps. And slowly I crawl back to the light.

Heifer at breakfast

I was filming in Torbay, doing a piece on seed companies, a number of which are based in the area. I had been working a great deal and Sarah and the children were away, staying with friends. I was tired and had started to notice the usual warning signs – weeping at news stories or finding certain sad songs looping over and over in my head, but this was not – is not – particularly unusual. It can be managed.

I was staying at one of the old wedding-cake hotels on the seafront and went down to breakfast early on a sunny autumn morning. The dining room was vast and almost empty with more waiters than guests. As I ate my cereal I looked up and saw a brown and white heifer lumber silently through the room, its back legs kicking sideways a little, almost skittish, but its eyes were scared.

I realised that no one else had seen it. It was mine.

A wave of intense sadness soaked through me. I felt completely alone. I sat quietly for a minute or two gathering myself, unable to move, letting the storm pass. All day I filmed amongst the seeds, knowing that I was not well, knowing that this was not good, knowing that if I let go, I might never put the pieces back together again.

I drove home, a grown man sobbing on the motorway, and got back to the empty house. I rang Sarah and from the other side of the country she lovingly talked me down, like a flight controller bringing a flaming plane safely in to land.

Something breaks. Something shatters, and it takes a long while to put it all together again.

Familiar ground

After an 18-month gap I began to garden again. Our new house had two acres of scrubby, abandoned field. I visited it almost every day and spent at least three months simply clearing the ground. All but the walled garden had been left untended for three or four years and I cut the grass, brambles, burdocks, thistles, docks and nettles three times that spring and summer, raking them all up by hand. Each operation took about a fortnight, but meant that at the most basic level I got to know the plot. This familiarity cannot be cheated. You need to discover where the sun falls or casts unlikely shadow, where the wind nips in and where a seemingly flat space has a fall unnoticed by the eye.

My mother comes from Herefordshire farming stock, so I suppose this place is in my blood, but I'm still aware of how lucky we are to live in this part of the world. We look across to scattered hamlets and timber-framed farms, sometimes with a grander red-brick front. I doubt if the pattern of settlement has changed much since the Roman invasion. We are surrounded by flat marshy farmland, with the hills of Radnor Forest in the distance. The willows and the alders dominate the spare watery landscape. Cattle feed on the rich spring grass of the water meadows and are fat and glossy by midsummer. The fields are enclosed with hawthorn hedges or the remnants of ancient woodland with elder, hazel, dogwood, ash and oak covered in honeysuckle and old man's beard. There are still mature orchards, undergrazed by sheep, which are so characteristic of Herefordshire. This has strongly influenced my approach to gardening, because I firmly believe that no man-made garden could look lovelier.

So we have made our garden wilder towards the boundary, using hawthorn and field maple hedges rather than the yew, hornbeam and holly of the more formal areas. Our little orchard with its rough grass is an echo of the old farm. I hate over-neat gardens with harsh edges, over-pruned shrubs and not a weed in sight. We have deliberately left clumps of stinging nettles as they are an important insect habitat. I love shagginess and abundance, and the jewel garden is planted on such rich soil that the plants grow taller than any description on the seed packet.

All the while that I was scything and raking I was scheming and dreaming, working myself into the place. They say that if you want something enough it will happen, but this is only half the story. Just wanting is not enough. You must dream it too. If you can dream every square inch of a garden, every day of its year and every flavour of its season, then you can make it happen.

Before I planted a thing I had a year of measuring, clearing and marking out with string and canes. After a few months I had a hologram of the garden I wanted clearly imposed on the empty mown space. I would use much of the time I spent lying awake each night working my way round this garden-to-be, and creating an intimacy that existence would only cement. All through the Nineties the garden was the touchstone by which I measured all the other things in my life. It ran like a river through all my thoughts, despite the fact that I had less and less time to give it.

Archaeology

Because the garden behind the house grew out of a field, we are always digging up old hinges, farm machinery and clenched nails. I am fascinated by the archaeology of the place. I have found hundreds of flints in the borders, yet this is not a flinty area – we have clay. Where do they come from? There is an Iron Age hill fort about a mile away; perhaps the people who lived in safety up there came down to the river to hunt and fish and left them here.

The farmhouse and field sit on a platform near a bend on the River Arrow. At times of flooding it is just high enough to remain dry. It is always astonishing to see acres of water to the north and west of us, stretching out like a great lake. Even during the terrible floods in 1994 and 2001 the house stayed as dry as a bone. When we first came here I was surprised that there was no cellar, and instead there was a cold windowless room, known as the cellar, at ground level. It is now obvious why the house did not have foundations deep enough for a cellar – because the water table is too high.

Sarah has collected all the hinges and other farm metalwork unearthed in the garden over the years.

When the granary steps were being repaired broken medieval encaustic tiles were found. One of them bore the religious inscription 'INRI'. It was almost as if they had been dumped there – perhaps they came from Leominster Priory with a load of stone on the back of a cart after the dissolution of the monasteries. But there is also evidence that there was a private chapel here in Tudor times.

At the front of the house we have simple grass and topiary – all green, no flowers at all. We think it suits the austerity of the front of the house, but the practical reason is the remains of medieval drains and the foundations of earlier buildings, at a slightly different alignment to the present house. We excavated this area and the finds were photographed by the county archaeologist – then carefully covered up with sand and grass planted over them.

Accusations

We moved in on 8th December 1992. The house was still a building site because we couldn't afford to pay the builders any more. We were completely, stony broke. For a while I had received no unemployment benefit because I had signed off to go camping with the children for a fortnight. When I returned to sign back on I was told that I was ineligible. We struggled by, flogging off bits and pieces of furniture in the local sale rooms whilst negotiating Kafkaesque bureaucracy. It turned out that they were not paying me anything – despite my position having not changed in any way – because someone had written an anonymous letter accusing me of secretly working, and although completely untrue and not supported by any evidence, payment had been stopped and we had been subject to an undercover fraud investigation for the previous three months. When we challenged this and went through yet more labyrinthian bureaucracy, the payments started again without any apology or explanation. Back payments were never made.

> The day we moved in was Tom's second birthday so we had a party, perched on packing cases with tea laid out on a wobbly wallpapering table. My parents had given us the best house-warming present possible – an ancient Aga which, once assembled and running, was my favourite spot in the house. While the rest of the house was unheated I spent as much time as possible resting the newspaper on top of it and keeping warm until the pages were too crisp to turn.

Turning a corner

That day the phone went – the first time a telephone had ever rung in that 500-year-old building. It was Granada, offering me studio work the following day. This was the first time they had contacted me in over six months. I went and did it, and the producer, who I had never met before, said I was pretty good at it, why didn't I do more? You learn that it is better to smile wryly than throttle

We seem cheerful enough but it was a difficult time. The winter honeysuckle in the pot is now a large bush.

such people. But it did lead to more work. I did endless makeovers – usually entirely alone, laying patios and digging borders between takes. I wrote freelance pieces for just about every paper, one of which was for the *Observer* detailing the traumatic experience of our benefit fraud accusation. The great Jane Bown came to take a picture of Sarah and myself, outside the front door. It beat the hell out of selling jewellery to Boy George, Michael Jackson or Princess Diana.

A week after this article was published I took a call from someone purporting to be from Hollywood. Before he could explain himself I put the phone down on what I assumed was a joke. He rang back immediately. He was an English director based in Los Angeles who read the *Observer* every week and wanted to make the story into a movie. He flew over to see us and paid me to write a script. It wasn't very good and never got made, but it was fascinating and fun and he paid me more than I had earned in the previous two years.

Gardening gold

By spring 1993 I had the garden more or less planned. I had done innumerable drawings and fixed woven fences wherever I wanted a hedge. Making these fences was one of the most enjoyable things I have ever done. The stakes – which for the 6-foot fences had to be 8 feet tall – were chestnut, and the woven material hazel. I was brought up in Hampshire where hazel coppices were common, but it turned out that most of Herefordshire's coppice had become overgrown and useless. Eventually I found a woodman who supplied me from a wood on the Shropshire border, and over the next couple of years he brought me thousands of 12-foot hazel rods. A neighbour came in and ploughed where we wanted our vegetables and when I saw the rich chocolate loam fall off the plough I knew that we had struck gardening gold. We could see that the earth beneath our feet was extraordinarily fertile. Next we needed plants.

> All our focus shifted on to the garden. One hundred pounds goes a long way in a garden but it is the cost of a couple of sockets or a radiator. Our apple store was built long before the airing cupboard. As fast as Montagu started to earn some money, it was spent on the garden rather than furniture. This has left us with an uncluttered house, which is probably an advantage, although a little austere.

Tree sale

In April 1993 a local tree nursery was giving up the lease of a field and was auctioning off all the remaining stock. Everything was to go – it would be cheaper to sell it at any price than shred it, let alone pot up and move hundreds of unwanted trees. It was the day of the Grand National and pouring with rain. By lunchtime everyone was wet through and most gave it up as a bad job. I stayed. I had gone intending to buy some yews and box. I came home having acquired over fifty large yews, a couple of dozen good-sized box, each of which would now cost hundreds of pounds, over fifty large lime trees, large field maples, cherries and ash as well as literally thousands of ash, hawthorn and field maple for hedging, 'Nevada' and *rugosa* roses by the bundle, dozens of good-sized Italian and common alders, scores of hollies and, rather oddly, some London planes. By mid-afternoon large trees were going for 50p each. I spent over a thousand pounds that we certainly did not have. I remember leaving a rain-soaked cheque and wondering if I would have time to persuade the bank to give me an overdraft before they got round to cashing it.

The huge pantechnicon that delivered them at dusk was unable to get down the track to our house, so the whole lot were dumped on the side of the road a quarter of a mile away. We were still shunting them down the lane at midnight.

But this provided us with the structure for the garden. We now had the material for two yew hedges, a holly hedge, mixed hedging right the way round the two acres, two long avenues of pleached limes, and yews and box for topiary.

This was a seminal moment, not least because it cost comparatively such an enormous sum of money that I felt honour-bound to make something of it. It also took the garden from a series of pored-over plans and notebooks full of lists and schemes into a reality that began to take on its own impetus. Gardens that are carefully designed and then enacted by rote have no soul. To come truly alive things have to happen of their own accord, out of synch with the best-laid plans. The huge quantity of nursery stock that I had impulsively bought dictated the feel and shape of the garden as much as my imagination.

Barns

This had been a working farm up until 1990 and the farmer had held on to a range of barns including hopkilns and stables, butting on to our house with a yard at the front and back. There was planning permission to turn them into two houses. Occasionally people would view them and I would feel a lurch in the pit of my stomach. We would have been completely overlooked. Although we had no means to buy them we started negotiations, and after a couple of years she agreed to sell them to us.

If we had had them from the very beginning, undoubtedly the garden would have been laid out differently. Not only did the barns give us much better access to the garden (for the previous three years our only way to the back had been through the house) but they also gave us tool and potting sheds that are almost as much a luxury as living space.

All our buildings fascinate me and have influenced the structure of the garden more than anything else. I have to relate the garden to the house, and the house to the garden. The view from a window will influence the positioning of a pathway and a doorway at the end of that path. I have a primitive need for symmetry and balance.

Architecture

I became increasingly aware that I had to earn a living if Montagu was ill again. Although I had worked as a designer all my life, I had no formal qualifications and the thought of designing jewellery again made me feel sick.

On August bank holiday 1993 I was lying in the bath and it struck me that I wanted to study architecture. If it was going to happen I had to start straight away. Within days I had an interview in Oxford and found myself enrolled to start an architectural degree. Over the next three years I struggled to combine commuting to Oxford three days a week, which was a four-hour round trip, with looking after three small children. This was a period in which Montagu was taking any and every job he could to repay our debts, meaning that he was away from home filming for half the year. I would often draw all night with the three children asleep in my bed, then leave at 6.30 for a 10 o'clock lecture. It was exhausting, stimulating, absorbing and I loved it. It is one of my greatest regrets that I did not qualify.

Travel

I became the *Observer*'s gardening editor in February 1994 and have written a weekly column for them ever since. It is the nearest thing to a proper job that I have ever had. In April that year, as well as the regular work for *This Morning* that continued right through to 1998, I started reporting for the BBC's *Holiday* programme. Over the next four years I made around eighty films for them, each one taking me away for about five days. Most of these trips involved travelling long distances and all were as disconnected from life at home as was imaginable. I would be somewhere like the Bahamas, Thailand or Corfu, filming in a five-star hotel whilst Sarah would be at home in a building site, trying to do her degree course with three small children to care for and bailiffs hammering at the door.

It was not the life we had planned or wanted. For fifteen years everything important had been done together and was as a result better than anything either could have done alone. Now we were sharing too little. My work supplied the money we desperately needed, but little else. I would often write an article about our precious garden from a hotel room on the other side of the world. Whilst I was standing on a beach somewhere I would always be thinking about home, whereas Sarah was left having to deal with the unglamorous realities of our world. One of the more absurd ironies was that I have always hated travelling, while Sarah loves it. Both of us envied and resented the other's position and yet, despite the slog of constant writing and filming and travelling, I undoubtedly had the softer option.

It was the middle of winter and I was lying in bed under a tarpaulin. Everywhere was filthy – the plaster dust made me cough all night – and the bedroom had no windows, just two gaping holes in the wall with another flappy, ineffectual tarpaulin fighting the weather. As I fell asleep there was a phone call from a bar in the Bahamas. I could hear laughter in the background and the offer of another drink. Montagu was ringing to say goodnight as he always did. He was sweet and loving and sympathetic, but I couldn't stop myself from thinking about the unfairness of my lot. The marriage was based on parity but it seemed that the balance was in Montagu's favour.

Balancing the books

Later that summer a bailiff arrived for the second time for a petty debt. I think it was for non-payment of a small amount of VAT. I hid from him, but from that moment I decided to take control of the finances and do what I could to improve our situation. I advertised for a part-time bookkeeper and her first job was to sort out a box of expense claims going back two years. Over the next couple of months she clawed back several thousand pounds, which made a huge difference. It was a corner turned.

Whilst television pays much less than most people realise, all this work meant that I was earning a good income. Slowly we paid off debts and were able to buy furniture as well as the tumbledown barns adjoining our house, which Sarah has restored.

The garden has been done on a shoestring by professional standards, but has still had a small fortune lavished upon it by most people's measures. I cannot think of anything that I would rather spend my money on.

Home

The integration of domesticity and work has been the most important part of being here. However, I need to get away occasionally to see the picture clearly, but because Montagu is away so much I can't leave very often. The children used to hate it when I went on trips with him. When they were little it seemed that they had no concept of how long a day was, let alone a week, and they missed us terribly if we didn't come home at night. So one of us had to be there.

I hate being confined, but Montagu can be happy not leaving the garden for days on end. He will scarcely notice. Almost all his inspiration and motivation is internal and self-generated. Most of my ideas have come to me by going into the outside world. I love London. To me it is a concentration of energy. I even love the smell of Paddington station, as I breathe in particulates and fumes. On the train there I plan out my day visiting galleries, shops, buildings. I am happiest alone. Once I've had my fix of the city I return refreshed and with a clear head. I often spend the journey back covering my yellow lined legal pad in drawings and notes, pouring a stream of ideas. It's always lovely to come home to find the fires burning and the children pleased to see me.

I stopped travelling so much in 1998 when I moved from the BBC to Channel 4. In 1999 Sarah and I wrote *Fork to Fork* together and made a series of the same name. This restored some integrity to our lives, collaborating on work that really mattered to us. Television still takes me away from home more than I would like, and when I am here I spend more time writing at my desk than outside in the garden. But to maintain my sanity I need at least one full day a week in the garden. It works better than any pill, better than any medicine. Earth heals.

Over the years life has become more comfortable and the happiest time that we spend together is in the garden. The energy has now gone from making it to sustaining its rhythm. In the morning, looking out of an upstairs window, I see Montagu striding through the garden, followed by the dogs, holding the steel bowl with scraps for the chickens. When he is away, which thankfully is nowadays not so often, I have to take over the opening of the greenhouses, the watering, the feeding of the animals in the morning, and then do it all again in the evening. It seems to take ages.

I have always loathed routine, yet I see it as part of the reason for his success as he manages to pack so much into his day. If he's writing a book he gets up at five and works until it's time to help get the children off to school. This is his most creative time.

There are rarely lie-ins in the Don household. As it is I never have enough time. I long to be able to wake up, throw on my old gardening clothes and go straight outside. But first we have to get over all the domestic hurdles. There is always so much to do and a constant sense of working against the clock. But I love it.

We have made this garden together; there is nothing in it that is not a result of that partnership. From the mess and joy of our past and present we have created a place that is intensely personal, yet lives quite separately from us. It is this precious thing that we are making out of life's muddle.

The garden

Monty: Although we have a specific area of the garden that is called the jewel garden, in fact its influence spreads right across our whole territory. So let me take you on a guided tour.

The path to the front door is flanked by 26 topiary yew cones set in a lawn. A tall yew hedge encloses it, making it an entirely evergreen, formal space. To one side is the walled garden, full of white and pastel flowers, with a large paved area where we eat outside. But most of the garden stretches out behind the house, which being set in the corner of a rectangle, involves going through the front door, out the back and turning sharp left.

When it came to planning the layout this was the first problem. I resolved it by making three parallel paths down the length of the garden, the central one taking you through all the various enclosures, and the outer two acting as corridors off them. More paths run at right angles across the garden. Using this grid I planted hedges and made separate spaces. The sinuous curve of the boundary hedge dictates that the outer compartments are irregular in shape and size, but I have no regrets about the grid-like nature of the plan.

The spring garden is directly opposite the back door, bounded on one side by the lime walk, by the field hedge on the other, and tapers from about ten paces wide to just one. The vegetable garden, jewel garden, coppice and cricket pitch (so called because about six summers ago we played cricket there

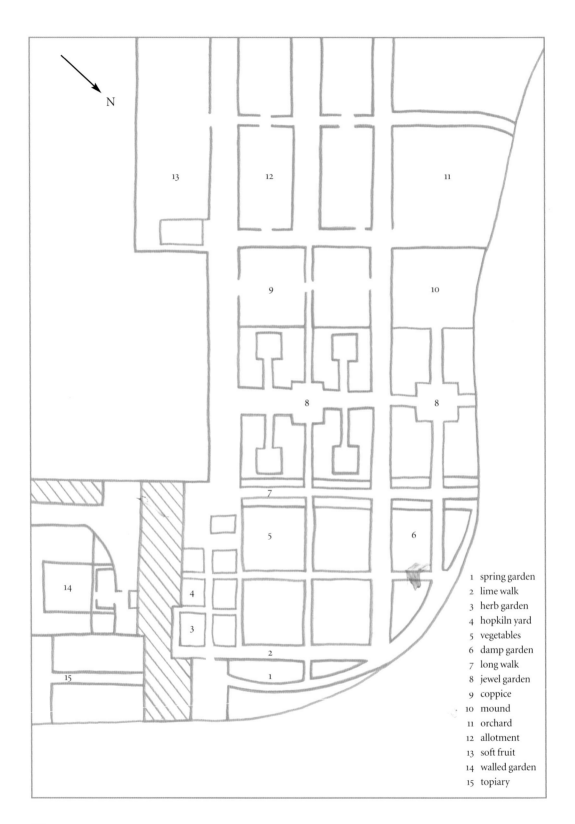

N

1 spring garden
2 lime walk
3 herb garden
4 hopkiln yard
5 vegetables
6 damp garden
7 long walk
8 jewel garden
9 coppice
10 mound
11 orchard
12 allotment
13 soft fruit
14 walled garden
15 topiary

a few times) all lie as consecutive enclosures down the centre of the garden. The herb garden, hopkiln yard and greenhouse yard run off each other to the south of the main gardens, and the damp garden, the lower part of the jewel garden and what we call the mound are on the other side of the central strip, to the north, bounded by the water meadow. The long walk runs right across the width of the entire garden, parallel to the lime walk, dividing the vegetable and jewel gardens.

A path runs between the jewel garden and our neighbours to the south and brings us to the soft fruit area, and the service area of the garden with nursery beds, compost heaps and suchlike. The orchard fills the rest of this top area and is bounded on two sides by a high hawthorn hedge.

Because of the corner position of the house there is no overview of the whole garden, just tantalising glimpses of parts of it. This makes it seem rather larger than it actually is.

The whole garden. It has evolved over the years but most of it was drawn out before anything was planted.

Growing jewels

Throughout the Eighties the combination of jewellery and gardening had dominated our lives. Both were, in their own ways, our embarrassment and our ruin. They certainly seemed incompatible and although we had no one to blame but ourselves, we had a powerful sense that jewellery had cost us the house and garden that we loved. So after the collapse of our company we shed it like a skin. It was something that other people with our names and address once did. But gradually we came to accept that this had been at the very least an interesting episode, and brought it back to the present through the jewel garden.

In the autumn of 1996 we decided to turn a circular lawn right in the centre of our plot into four grassed areas each with a woven willow house with hops trained over it. We divided the areas with hornbeam-lined paths, but quickly realised that we had made a mistake. But while the hop-houses were easy to shift, the paths and hedges were more permanent. So we decided to make flowerbeds where the grass had been, without really knowing what we wanted them to do.

You might ask why flowers should do anything at all? But in a garden context is everything. No plant has meaning unless it relates to its neighbouring plants, hedges and trees, paths, walls or fences, surrounding buildings and even the quality of the light. Especially the light. What looks great under a Californian or Mediterranean sky can look stranded further north.

> *Sarah*: As the plan began to be laid out by Montagu, with individual gardens enclosed by woven hazel fences that protected young hedging plants, the structure dominated everything. The paths were made, vegetables planted, topiary placed, an orchard planned but . . . there was an absence of flowers. We planted herbaceous borders on the outside of the vegetable garden. They were pretty in a cottage garden kind of way. But they were not enough. I wanted somewhere where flowers dominated.
>
> The jewel garden was an idea that had floated after us for several years. At last we got round to making it real. The area we chose for it had already had several incarnations, as a chicken run, a circular lawn, and latterly as four hornbeam enclosures.
>
> What I really wanted was a double border spanning the entire width of the garden. The general effect would be that of a long border even if it was crossed by paths. The only time I visited Great Dixter, Christopher Lloyd's masterpiece in Sussex, I was bowled over by his Long Border. I loved the clashing colours and the sheer theatrical scale of it, with everything – trees, shrubs, annuals – mixed in a glorious abundance.

There were ghosts to be laid. The whole experience of the collapse of our business and loss of our home had left a wound. It was hardly a tragedy, but it had hurt. One way of coping was to bury the past and get on with the present as best we could. Many people had asked if we would ever go back to making jewellery but the prospect was unthinkable. However, making a jewel garden did seem a good idea. The flowers would rise sparkling from the ashes of our past.

The initial area of what was to become the jewel garden was about twenty by twenty yards, which, by the time that you account for paths and hedges, still left over two thousand square feet to grow flowers in.

The first jewel garden, around 1996.

When we used to design a jewellery collection we always chose a theme and stuck with it right through to the last detail. We approached the jewel garden in the same way. We had a theme and would stick to it. We divided this square area into eight rectangular borders like this:

| PASTELS | JEWEL |
| CRYSTAL AND GOLD | JEWEL |

HORNBEAM TUNNEL

| CRYSTAL AND GOLD | BRIGHTS |
| PASTELS | BRIGHTS |

Each pair of borders was to be self-contained whilst relating within the overall theme to the other three. Throughout we would use jewel colours or associations in our combination of plants.

From the start it did not all go to plan. The extra width of the central path was the result of a cock-up. We had hired a bobcat and driver to shift the vast pile of rubble our ongoing building work had accumulated. Looking at our new garden plans, he suggested laying it as hardcore for the paths. This sounded ideal.

I had already planted part of the central path with hornbeams with the intention of training them into a tunnel, which I planned to extend later. But I forgot to tell the bobcat driver of this future development. Sarah and I went out for an hour or two leaving him to get on with it and when we returned he had carefully lined up the edge of the new path with the existing hornbeams so it was at least three foot wider than we wanted. This put paid to any plans for extending the hornbeam tunnel. With no less than three feet of compacted rubble buried beneath it, to narrow it down would have meant hiring a digger or a backbreaking week with pick, shovel and a barrow. Which is why this path is so much wider than any other in the garden.

Preparing the borders was a slog. It took all winter. We were attempting the biggest project so far in the garden. When we made the vegetable garden – which is smaller anyway – it had been cultivated with a large tractor and reversible plough. But that was before we had planted any hedges or trees. But now the biggest piece of kit that we could get in to help us was a Rotovator. So all the digging had to be done by hand.

First we had to lift the turf. There was a lot of the stuff and this took days and days of slow, hard graft, although it was a good excuse for using my grandfather's turfer, a kind of giant spatulate ace of spades. I discovered to my cost that turf lifting has its own particular injury, a graze along the right forearm caused by repeatedly pushing horizontally under the turf across your bended right knee. You can keep your sleeves buttoned down of course but if you are like me you don't think about it until the damage is done.

Once the bare soil was revealed I dug it over mixing in thirty tons of well-rotted cattle manure. This was all done at evenings and weekends. I would come back from filming some joyride in the Caribbean, take off the fancy suit, lace up my boots, go outside and get back to the real work. It was a strange mixed-up life. But the slog was fuelled by the poetry of the plan: a garden full of jewels growing out from ground that we had painstakingly tended.

> We agreed that one of the four spaces should be planted only in amethyst, sapphire, ruby and emerald. No yellow of any kind, no oranges, lilacs, mauves or browns. This restriction would be creative. The emerald could be provided by richly green leaves. The reds should be essentially ruby which could embrace scarlets and crimsons but try to exclude any hint of pink.
>
> Amethyst, or purple, was easy. We already had crocus, violas, irises, clematis, geraniums, alliums, buddleias and purple hazel in the garden and they could be moved to this new site. We also had standard hollies left over from the tree sale, adding structure, year-round emerald and winter ruby berries. Sapphire, or blue, would be hard to represent as strongly as the other three colours, but delphiniums, cornflowers, *Salvia patens*, asters and *Anchusa azurea* 'Loddon Royalist' were all to hand and further blues could be nurtured and cajoled.

What should go in the other three quarters? We changed our minds a dozen times. *Holiday* filming trips came and went and the ground was steadily turned over before we realised that we were overlooking the obvious (which is consistently our biggest failing). We had taken our 'Jewel' colours from the language of the costume jewellery trade. The four colour groups that everyone in that business uses are known as 'Jewel', 'Pastels', 'Brights' and 'Crystal'. On one level they are bits of jargon but they still directly related to the world in which we had worked. In a garden based on our bejewelled past, these rather daft expressions had meaning and could easily be applied to flowers.

So 'Jewel' colours included rich purple, blue, red and green. 'Pastels' included all pinks, soft blues, lilacs, mauves and soft yellows. 'Brights' translated into oranges, lime greens, magenta, and any tone of colour jazzy in its own right but shockingly so when clattered in with other fizzers. The gaudy mix of oranges, reds, magentas and greens is nowadays trendy but in 1996 it was considered by most people full-on bad taste. 'Crystal' refers to the clear sparkly stones which we had nearly always used in conjunction with silver. Obviously though in floral terms this does not means 'clear' but white.

White, but not quite. We had to have a token of gold and silver. If silver went with the pastels in the shape of grey plants such as cardoons, plume poppies, mulleins, artemisia and onopordums, then gold could go with the white making a Crystal and Gold garden.

> We had to choose flowers that were golden rather than yellow. Garden snobs seem to find some yellows beyond the pale, which is absurd, but we found ourselves having to distinguish between the different tones of yellows, choosing richer ones for the jewel garden and selecting softer, lemony yellows like mulleins and the pale yellow marguerite *Anthemis tinctoria* 'E.C. Buxton' for the walled garden.

The planting got going in the spring and summer of 1997. Given the quality of our soil and the astonishing speed with which any border gets established here, by August the concept felt tangible. This was exciting.

But it was not coming together as we had intended. There were crude limitations, particularly with our plants, not least because the majority were either moved from other parts of the garden or grown from seed. Although this meant that they were all free, not all were appropriate. A free plant in the wrong place still looks wrong. So that winter we went back to the drawing board.

We decided that the planting was too fussy and disparate and – other than the fact that they were all based on obscure jewellers' jargon – they might as well have been four quite separate back gardens. It all needed opening out and integrating. So in the beginning of 1998 I removed the four hedges that divided the four areas, making one big enclosure. We then added four access paths to the four that already existed so we were now left with sixteen smaller square beds. The idea was to make the jewel garden seem like four huge square borders, crossed by wide central paths.

Our early attempts at planting had been too complex and didn't quite work, so we simplified the palette. Pale colours were banished and each bed was connected to the next by rich colours, giving a sense of continuity.

I have learned that one secret of a good border is to make it as deep as possible. Our borders are edged with box and the flowers spill over but are contained. The rigour of the clipped box is in contrast with the abundance of the beds. At knee height these box hedges are deliberately rather taller than most edging plants because we wanted to create the impression of a jewel box overflowing with precious plants.

However, this adds a level of complexity because it means that we cannot have any low plants in the front of a border because they would be hidden by the hedge. But it has the counter effect of bringing tall plants to the front so that in high summer, as you walk past, the edge of each border is a sheer cliff of colour towering over you. Another unexpected side effect of this planting is that the hazy tangle of flowers is very hard to capture in a photograph.

The evolving layout of the jewel garden: 1997 (top), 1999 (middle) and 2004 (bottom).

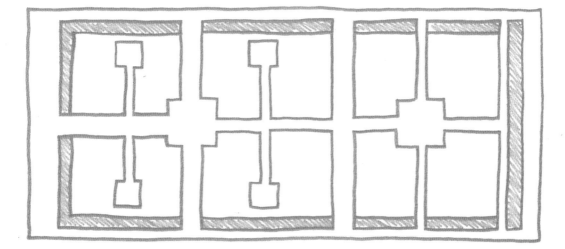

But that is getting ahead of ourselves. First we had to order a lot of plants. For us this was a big step. Up until then our plant buying had been restricted to structural plants and occasional bits and pieces bought on a whim. Now that the internal hedges had gone we needed height so we added a pair of *Robinia pseudoacacia* 'Aurea', a laburnum and wigwams of hazel to support clematis and sweet peas. We bought a pair of weeping silver pears, more cardoons, macleaya, and grasses such as *Festuca glauca* and *Deschampsia cespitosa* 'Goldtau'.

Of the four themes, the 'Jewel' colours had worked best, the fantastic rich plum colour of opium poppies providing first-year intensity and *Knautia macedonica*, chocolate cosmos, crocosmia and *Geum* 'Mrs J. Bradshaw' being particularly successful. But, despite our careful and sophisticated plant choices, the best splash of intense colour came from a type of spinach that had sneakily self-seeded itself from the vegetable garden. This was red orache, *Atriplex hortensis*, and it has remained one of the mainstays of the garden. In fact we pull up barrow-loads of the stuff every year to stop it taking over.

The 'Brights' section looked good too but perhaps this was simply because it was so visible. Nasturtiums, marigolds, the geranium 'Ann Folkard' all sashayed through the late summer. But it was the area that stood most apart from the rest.

Still, we felt that we were on to something. It was starting to come together. But we should have kept quiet about it, been patient and modest, and waited a few years before showing it to anyone.

Loose talk

I had to give a talk to the Horticultural Society of New York, and decided at the last minute to mention this project that was consuming us. I used some highly selective and flattering pictures that Sarah had taken in midsummer. The light in the lecture hall was rather bright, which meant that even the broad outline of the pictures projected behind me could scarcely be seen, let alone any detail.

So what the audience lacked in visual images I supplied with words, swiftly moving from embellishment to invention. The garden I described was rich with a wide range of plants, all in perfect condition, and all flowering exactly when and how we wanted, the succession and combinations dancing and glowing with true jewel-like intensity. It was a garden that I fervently wished to see and that we truly intended to make but alas which bore little resemblance to one that had ever existed – let alone our immature plot back in England.

This flight of fancy resulted in an eminent gardening editor asking to feature this wonderful jewel garden in American *House & Garden* the following summer. To my dismay I heard myself agree. But at that stage our jewel garden was not worth the trip from London, let alone the States. As we faced the December reality of mud and bare earth we realised with a too-familiar drowning feeling that either we had to eat humble pie and put it off or do something fast and pull it off. I did start on the humble-pie route and made a phone call, but they merely took this as a delightful example of British modesty and firmed up the dates.

Montagu's lecture at that charity lunch had been a surreal experience filled mainly with women in head-to-toe Chanel and lifted, tucked, primped and pumped. I was dressed for a casual talk and felt entirely out of place but it was fascinating. A few weeks later the *House & Garden* journalist came to stay with her husband and saw the garden. We all instantly clicked and became friends. It was winter and the shortcomings of the barely extant jewel garden were hidden.

That spring Montagu was as busy as ever and one night at the beginning of May I woke with a start and realised the concept had to become a reality. It *had* to look fabulous by August. I estimated that annual seeds took ten to twelve weeks to flower so if they were sown immediately we might just be able to get the garden to look good enough in time. Luckily the sweet peas had been sown in mid-February, and these would give important height and colour on their tripods. I had put in a large order to Thompson & Morgan and these seeds had arrived and were ready to be sown.

At the time we were also very busy writing and filming *Fork to Fork* which was about everything *but* the jewel garden. Montagu was also away filming for Channel 4 most of the week and always had at least one article to write at the weekend. It was down to me to make sure that it was ready on time.

We ditched the costume jewellery categories of Crystal, Brights, Pastels and Jewel. They had got us going but were now proving too limiting. We moved all white and pastels to the walled garden. We found ourselves again having to make rather arbitrary decisions. When is yellow gold? When does red become pink? Even more confusingly, when does magenta – which is acceptably jewel-like – become pink? Do we keep variegated plants? What if a plant has pastel flowers but perfectly jewel-like foliage?

The previous year we had grown far more sweet peas than we really needed or wanted so had put up 24 eight-strutted wigwams, more to use the laboriously propagated and potted-up plants than anything else, and these had been the hit of the summer, providing colour, scent and structure. They had also provided one of the best memories of the year, of seeing our beautiful daughter walking through the garden carrying enormous bunches of sweet peas for the house. And of course, the more sweet peas are picked, the more flowers they produce.

So we selected their seed carefully, mainly from Peter Grayson's excellent catalogue, sticking to the darker or most intense colours like 'Black Diamond', 'Midnight' and 'Black Knight', which are all dark maroons, the highly scented red 'Gypsy Queen', *Lathyrus chloranthus*, which has lime-green flowers, and perhaps our favourite, 'Cupani's Original'.

For the first time we planted grasses in the border. I had bought a variety of *Stipa gigantea* that was a more delicate golden form than the usual thugs. We increased the metallic feel throughout, broadening the range to include bronze, brass and copper as well as the existing gold and silver.

We planted brown grasses such as the carexes *comans*, *flagellifera* and *kaloides* mingling with the apricot foxglove, *Digitalis ferruginea*, the poppy 'Patty's Plum' and the rusty brown heleniums like 'Moerheim Beauty' and the annual sunflowers shot with velvet brown such as 'Velvet Queen' or 'Prado Red'.

To create an instant impression, we planted in clumps of five or seven plants, being more sparing only with the bright oranges and magentas.

Our biggest investment of all to impress the American cameras was enough box plants to edge the main crossing paths. Buying these went against the grain as until then all our box had been taken from cuttings, but it gave us about four years' start on our own stock – now, five years later, these plants make a foursquare, ageless hedge.

I was so busy that summer that the jewel garden had to be satisfied in snatched moments as and when they were available. We probably spent more on plants that summer than we had in all our previous gardening years put together as we dressed the borders in their finery. It was like having a mistress. I imagine. Oh, and we had builders working on the house throughout the whole period too.

Three days were booked for the photoshoot at the beginning of August. This was to catch the ideal moment before things began their gradual slide into autumn. But it was a very hot and dry July and our plants were going over fast.

This is from my garden diary, which Sarah keeps up when I am away:

31st July. Whole of July hot and sunny. Best month's weather for four years. Rained only twice. Ground parched and dusty.

1st August. Extremely hot. Became humid. Storm at teatime – first rain since 19th. We planted 12 Cosmos atrosanguineus *and 24* Crocosmia *'Dusky maiden'. Dead-headed. Watered. Huge rainstorm at 5.30 pm. Sarah worked in jewel garden 7-10 pm cutting back ligularias, staking and tidying. Garden never lovelier.*

Montagu went away for four days and I took over the diary – along with everything else:

2nd August. Builders arrived – two plasterers, carpenter, driver plus boy – chaos – taking down scaffolding. Four pallets of lime plaster delivered and blocking lane at 8.30am.

Staking, tying back, raking paths, picking sweet peas – so much to do. Went to garden centre in search of agapanthus – NONE. Bought:

3 x lyme grass (v. invasive)
3 x Miscanthus sinensis *'Morning Light'*
3 x Salvia farinacea
2 x Nepeta sibirica *'Souvenir d'André Chaudron'*

Swirling gusty wind at 5 pm, sky darkening. Thunderstorm which flattened everything. DISASTER.

3rd August. DISASTER – <u>storm has flattened garden</u> – despair. <u>Everything sodden</u>, <u>rotten</u> petals keeling over. Gareth came with girlfriend Sarah and set task of repairing damage. All day tying, staking, cutting off damaged flowers. Girlfriend Sarah on sweet pea duty. Gareth and Tom on artichokes and cardoons.

We are short of pea sticks. NEXT YEAR I VOW TO STAKE EVERYTHING PROPERLY EARLY.

Went to Hereford and clutch went on car. Freya and I got lift back in Robin Reliant along with very large jolly lady and three enormous dogs.

Worked till 8.30 pm raking, tidying, emptying wheelbarrows. I think it can be saved. If we blitz it all day tomorrow it might be okay. Then made children supper and cheered us all up with champagne.

4th August. George & Rose, Gareth and girlfriend, myself, Sarah Pearson, Fred and Jim all tidied garden all day. The garden has never had so much concentrated work, let alone such minute pampering. Between us all we propped and primped every single plant, swept every inch of path and clipped and tidied every stray leaf or blade of grass. The wreckage of 24 hours ago is almost completely rescued or hidden.

I came home just before dark that night and, blissfully unaware of the events that had taken place in my absence, took my customary walk around the garden. It seemed to be pretty much as I had left it, although I could see that there had been some final tidying up for the shoot. When I told Sarah this at supper she threw a plate at my head. Normally she is a pretty good shot but utter exhaustion sent it wide of the mark.

As it turned out the shoot, although tense, was successful. The pictures looked great and the article was very flattering.

Flux

In 2000 we made more changes to the jewel garden, removing the narrow access paths that had originally divided the four separate sections and extending it all by another third down into an area that had been where the chickens lived. There was nowhere else for it to go. Only the boundary of our land halted its march.

In the autumn of that year we had almost constant rain and the garden flooded for two months, the water lapping over a sizeable section of the garden.

When the floods cleared we needed to do a lot of remedial work on paths and installed a new drain, which meant digging trenches right across the garden.

Apart from the walled garden, which from the first was where we often ate outside, the garden had always been a place of work, not a place just to be. There was nowhere to perch with a cup of tea, or balance the radio. I thought that we could make a little paved area, two yards square, in the middle of each of the four borders of the jewel garden. Each has room for a couple of chairs and some sort of table or large stone. I often sit there with my eyes closed, surrounded by flowers, listening to the song of dozens of thrushes, blackbirds and fearless robins.

In the lower section of the jewel garden, which we added a few years ago, Montagu planted four pleached limes, each in the corner of a square, which have been trained on to hazel rods. They are as high as the width of the paved area below them, forming a cube. This has made a marvellous place to sit looking out over the river. In the evening, when the light is low in the west, all the plants are backlit. The tall grasses, the *Rosa moyesii*, which we encourage to grow as vigorously as possible, and the giant Scotch thistles, all look especially good at this end of the garden, which is deliberately planted to be wilder and looser as it approaches the boundary.

We started planting tulips and alliums in December 1999 and have added thousands every year since. We have tried not to be too 'tasteful' with our choice and have gone mainly for the bright and brash colours. The tulips are now a big event in the garden and start the jewel garden's floral year in April.

Gradually we increased the box edging from cuttings to make a hedge to line all the paths. In October 2002 the box plants put in for the American shoot had their first topping off; immediately the garden in winter was transformed and given shape.

The hardest aspect of gardening on this scale is to keep the momentum going. Capricious weather and seed failure can ruin the best-planned designs. I am glad that there is no public access to the garden as we can make our mistakes in private. We often have failures, nothing is static. Working on the jewel garden is the same as any design process. All choices are reductions and much is rejected and all ideas are constantly honed.

The garden is in a state of constant flux. There is never a point to arrive at, other than the moments when we stop and simply take it all in. We both think about our garden all the time and it is so deeply entrenched into our lives that sometimes it is hard to know where the garden begins and we end.

Early spring

Spring starts for us on 15th February. This is Sarah's birthday and we have had enough of winter by then. It will often be freezing cold or bleakly wet. No matter. Whatever the weather, this is the start of a new year for Sarah and the garden and me.

Best of all there is a real sense of the days lengthening. By the end of February it is light by seven in the morning and remains light enough to stay outside until six in the evening. These extra moments are precious. Spring is peeking over the horizon.

We take stock of what seeds we have, including those we collected from the garden at the end of last summer, those that we failed to sow the previous year and those that we have got round to ordering.

There is always a temptation to cram the greenhouse with seedlings by the end of February, but most of the tender annuals like tithonia, leonotis, cosmos, salvias, nasturtiums or sunflowers, all to be planted out in the jewel or walled gardens, are best left until March. Otherwise we end up in April and May with extra potting-on to do and cold frames overcrowded with plants that still need protection against late frosts. So we hold back a little.

I like to have a sort out on the first sunny day of spring. It feels like sharpening my pencils before starting to draw. This usually happens while Montagu is pruning and I am happy for it to be my job as I like the sense of order it brings. So I sort out the clay pots and prepare them for planting, tidy the potting shed, have a bonfire, clean up around the greenhouse yard, weed any of the overwintering plants in the cold frames, such as agapanthus or salvias, and generally get the place ready for action. It is my way of reconnecting with the garden for a new year.

27th February. Dawn chorus started at 6.21 am. Heard the first curlew,
the first wallflowers came out and I mowed all the grass. It got dark almost
exactly at 6.15 pm.

The curlews always arrive sometime between Valentine's Day and the end of the month and their throaty, bubbling call curves thrillingly out of the darkness.

The birds sense spring early. Our nights are almost silent, especially just before dawn. The owls hoot and screech from the willows by the river and three miles away the Cardiff train clatters by every couple of hours. Every car is the exception that proves that there is no traffic in this corner of the Herefordshire night. So the dawn chorus edges out of an empty black space. It is tentative – almost fragile – in the middle of February, but by the time the clocks change it is a roaring hallelujah.

On early spring days when the sun streams through the windows my blood warms up and I start to move out of my winter lethargy. I must have been a lizard in another life. I am so affected by sunlight that within minutes my mood changes and everything is hopeful.

Unfortunately sunlight does not always coincide with crucial gardening periods. Seeds have to be sown and plants planted when the time is right. At this time of year the weather can veer madly from ice and snow to balmy sunshine in a day. So how you dress in the garden really matters. I have worked out a system starting with a long-sleeved T-shirt to protect my arms from scratches, an old cashmere jersey with a sleeveless fleece or jerkin on top. I wear loose trousers, long socks and proper boots. I make sure I have plenty of pockets. Then as the sun comes out I gradually peel layers off. Once I've got my boots on I feel ready for action. I have a lovely orange wheelbarrow that always has my set of tools ready: a small border fork and spade, a rake, Felco No. 2 secateurs, a trowel, a recycled rubber trug, tarred string, green rubber gloves and a notebook and pencil. I hate it if anyone else uses them – not that this seems to put anyone off. Perhaps I should be fiercer.

So, in my boots, wheeling my mobile toolkit, followed by Poppy, our ancient Jack Russell – who is always excited, for reasons best known to her, by a wheelbarrow – I can begin. The task may simply be weeding or transplanting seedlings, but invariably it brings with it a sense of calm and pleasure that I hope won't be interrupted – although it always is.

The primroses are at their softly astonishing best by the end of February. This, of course, is a feast that is moving earlier and earlier. Which is fine by me. I cannot have them soon enough. But the days when they were the Easter flower have probably gone for good. We move any that seed themselves around the garden into the coppice and in parts of it the spread is now an unbroken carpet beneath the hazel. The violets, and a little later, wood anemones interweave amongst them.

8th March. Beautiful morning. Birds singing 5.45. Light by 6.00.
- *Primroses <u>fantastic</u> but starting to grow out*
- *Violets starting*
- *Snowdrops almost completely gone (but took only a week to go from everything to nothing)*
- *Imperial fritillaries smelling foxy*
- *Tulips all showing*
- *First snowflake*
- *Hawthorn breaking all over the place but oddly irregular*

Hellebores are the most impressive plants of February and March, with none of the coyness or delicacy that so many spring flowers seem to possess. They are

The Corsican
hellebore,
*Helleborus
argutifolius.*

stately and confident, and considered terribly grown up and tasteful. But despite these handicaps you cannot fail to be charmed by them, especially *Helleborus orientalis*, holding their astonishing faces to the ground. The only way to really look at them is to lift each flower head between two fingers or to pick and float them in a shallow bowl of water.

Almost all our hellebores are in the spring garden and form the bulk of the planting in these months. We have some particularly dark Ballard strains in the jewel garden but they can look a little lost and isolated in the otherwise dormant borders. This is a classic case of colour coding becoming a rod for one's back. They are a wonderful rich plum colour so fulfil the jewel-like remit, but hellebores look best en masse and these would certainly enrich their slightly less exalted cousins fifty yards away in the spring garden.

We should really root out all the rather muddy pink seedlings that have self-hybridised because on the whole the nearer to white or black a hellebore flower can be the better it is. We have enough stunning 'pure' varieties to remind me of this every year but I have not the heart for the necessary ethnic cleansing. I like their profligacy and promiscuity, and the way that they grow in a clutter and jumble of sepia-edged pink. Anyway, I am more interested in the way a plant makes me feel than the purity of its provenance.

19th March. Sarah planted out teasels in the jewel garden, moved thalictrum and onopordums.

Goldfinches love teasels and occasionally I catch them balancing on the bristly heads greedily pulling at the seeds. We leave as many seed heads as possible for the birds but these are now all long eaten. Cutting back everything that has been left over winter is a sign that spring is here. We clear miscanthus, teasels and cardoons to let the new growth come through.

Neither lamb nor lion, March is a contrary month. The garden becomes a meteorological playground. We can gain a mass of growth from a fortnight of soft March weather – and then it can hold completely static for a fortnight in April. Unpredictability is the only certainty.

I prune the roses, late-flowering clematis and buddleias on the first convenient date after 15th February. Why? It would be easy to say that this is because it is late enough that there will not be too much soft growth to be blasted by late frosts and yet early enough for the same soft new growth to make plenty of new wood for flowering buds. But the truth is that Sarah's birthday is a door in the calendar that I unthinkingly go through. If it were 1st March or 30th January I would prune with the same solemn zeal.

I sow the sweet peas in February. We have tried sowing them as early as October but they just sit in their pots for months and do not seem to give us any more flowers. I normally sow about 150 four-inch pots, three seeds to a pot and put them in a cold frame to germinate. This sounds a lot but in early May we plant a pot at the base of each of the six hazel uprights of each wigwam. As we have between twenty and thirty sweet pea wigwams set around the garden, they soon get used up. I see no point in sweet peas without scent even if the colour is perfect for its place – but Montagu and I often argue about this.

Near here are the famous wild daffodil fields and woods at Dymock and you often see naturalised daffodils growing in old orchards around here. So five years ago we planted 100 wild daffodils to naturalise in our orchard but they are spreading very slowly and the last count was only around 50 flowers. We have also just planted 100 Tazetta daffodils 'Soft Cheerfulness' in the coppice, to carry on the soft yellow as the primroses fade.

I spread the self-sown seedlings of forget-me-nots and lime-green feverfew between the emerging clumps of tulips. One of my favourite things at this time of year is the unexpected combination of seedlings like red orache, poppies, marigolds and nigella with the odd cerinthe and sweet pea that have made it through the winter. I know that they need thinning but I leave them as long as possible so they look like a luxuriant carpet. I would rather have too many plants than too much bare earth.

Before I start work I often spend ages just looking at the garden. I might be focusing on a single plant or working out how to make more general changes in a border. Sometimes this will involve shifting or dividing plants or seeing where there is a gap to be filled. This constant tweaking is what keeps the garden fluid. The borders never remain the same from year to year.

If the soil is ready then March is a good time to plant and move things around. But 'ready' means dry enough and – critically – warm enough. The only rule is one of thumb – my thumb testing this soil in my hand today. There is a temptation to add plants because you have seen them in similar situations in pictures. But the right thing in the right place at the wrong time is still always going to look wrong.

In the damp garden the furled spikes of hostas push through the soil at the beginning of March. This is the best time to divide them, digging them up as a single heavy lump of root before chopping slices like cake, each with a spike or at least one visible bud. In this way, without really trying, we have gone from about a dozen to over fifty good-sized hostas, in under five years.

Mulching the jewel garden is a big job that has to be done no later than early March. If it is left after that the tulips are bashed and flattened however carefully you try and work round them. I used to believe that you should ideally wait until the soil was warm but I am not convinced that this makes any difference in the scheme of things. The best time to mulch is when you have

finished all moving and planting, and it is neither raining nor frozen. In practice there are not many days when the borders are ready and we have the mulching material to hand together with the time and right weather. Or inclination. It could be any time between November and March.

Over the years we have used three materials as mulch – garden compost, mushroom compost and cocoa shells. Each has a different effect and different pros and cons. Garden compost has most nutrition, is free and is the most effective at suppressing weeds. If we had enough I would use nothing else. Mushroom compost is weed free and very good for loosening our heavy clay soil. Cocoa shells are really easy to pour into place and also lighten a heavy soil, creating a curiously suet-like texture. We have ended up using a rotating combination of all three over the past four or five years. Mulching is slow, repetitive work, taking about forty working hours to cover just the jewel garden and perhaps double that for all the borders. But at least you can see what you have done.

Note the tulips and foliage: the pruning of the pleached limes was exceptionally late when this picture was taken. It is normally done in February.

*21st **March**. Frost and fog overnight. Became astonishing day – not a cloud and really hot sunshine. Worked all day in damp garden, digging, weeding, planting. Sat in sunshine with Sarah. Heaven.*

Mowed in afternoon. Outside till 6.30, red sun see-sawing against full moon in east.

Despite the intense anticipation there are days – sometimes weeks – when spring holds back. But always the hawthorns begin to break by the end of March. Not much in this life is better than the way that the first hawthorn leaves seem to float above the twiggy hedges for a week or so.

The most exciting day of the gardening year falls on the last weekend of March when the clocks, and the garden, go forward into the light.

Late spring

The last week of March until Whitsun – or 28th May, our eldest son Adam's birthday – is the best period of the year. Of course statements like that are hostages to fortune, but little can spoil the party. Every day has more light, more weather, more growth and more to do. The grass needs a weekly cut and the weeds grow with astonishing vigour. There is a lot of sowing to be done and inevitably that carries with it a train of thinning, pricking out, potting on, hardening off and planting out. Although there is much to do, the time and energy that comes from light and sunshine is equal to any demands.

The dawn chorus gets all the popular acclaim but the evening chorus as dusk falls at the end of March is just as exhilarating and, as it dies away, much more poignant. When I was a student my father made a tape recording of the evening chorus and sent it to me. I listened to it in my city lodgings, drunk on birdsong and Irish whiskey, tears rolling down my maudlin cheeks.

The imperial fritillary and 'White Triumphator' tulips in the spring garden.

The snakeskin fritillaries appear by the beginning of April, running alongside the path in the spring garden, no two the same in their patchwork colours. This area of flood-ground is ideal for them and they return every year without fuss, spreading gently. A few weeks later the imperial fritillaries flower. They rise out of the ground like a carnival float on an apparently modest flare of pale green leaves splaying off a central chocolate stem, before unfolding into an extraordinary pineapple head of orange-yellow flowers. Fully grown the whole performance stands five feet tall or more. We have lutea, which has yellow flowers, and rubra, which is a deep orange red. You plant the bulb in autumn on its side, the pointed end horizontal to the ground. It stinks of rancid tomcat or fox, even a touch of ordure. Yet at a distance it is surprisingly intoxicating.

Whilst my relationship with primroses is simple – I just adore them – I could get purist about cowslips. I am not sure that they are a garden plant. They belong to open fields, or wide grassy verges on country lanes. In fact the best cowslips I have seen are by the busy A4110. Flowers are no respecter of expectations. Ours were planted as plugs into the long grass bounding the orchard and overlap the primroses by a week or so, catching their early cousins' tail end.

Early April brings damson blossom, with light touches of small flowers scattered on scrawny little hedgerow trees, impossibly gay and spritely in a still pretty barren landscape. I have seen it lining snowy fields not looking at all out of place or season.

The spring garden in late April. The ancient hazel was the only tree in the garden when we arrived in 1991.

———————————

The spring garden shifts from flowers that are harbingers of spring but really belong to winter, like snowdrops, crocus, hellebores and primroses. By mid-April there are pulmonarias, forget-me-nots, daffodils, snowflakes, *Euphorbia polychroma*, *Clematis alpina*, the first tulip 'West Point', the little yellow flowers of *Ribes odoratum* and voluptuous crab apple blossom. The hellebores, although still fully in flower, are suddenly shunted from centre stage. They linger for a few more weeks but have lost their power.

Hanging out the washing one bright April day at one of our lowest points I heard the first cuckoo and realised that, however mundane, this was a sublime moment. Around this time we start to sit outside. Coffee, even lunch on an exceptional day, gets taken out into the spring sun. A picnic at Easter feels like a holiday.

On election day in May 1997 I was staying with my old friend Sarah Raven and her garden was full of technicolour tulips. I had never seen tulips grown with such intensity and it was a great inspiration. A couple of years later we made our first really substantial bulb order.

OVERLEAF Orange tulips in the jewel garden, late April. In the foreground are 'Orange Favourite', in the background 'Generaal de Wet'. The hollies are 'Golden Queen'.

In the jewel garden the earlier tulips – especially 'Queen of Sheba', 'Abu Hassan', 'Generaal de Wet', 'Rococo' and 'Prinses Irene' – really begin. Others follow on,

opening daily. There are the parrots – Black, Flaming, Blue and Orange;
more oranges – 'Orange Artist' and 'Orange Favourite' – purple 'Negrita', and
vermillion 'Ballerina', and the last to hit its stride is the almost black 'Queen of
Night'. For a few days at the cusp of April and May, all are zinging out at once.

The pear blossom peaks just as the earliest apple peeps into flower.
The white pear flowers start out leafless and then stay long enough for the
leaves to take over. A baton exchanged. I wish I had an old pear orchard, trees
as big as beeches, covered in flower against a blue April sky. There is nowhere
I ever want to be more than my garden in spring.

14th April. Shirtsleeve weather. The sheer luxury of it.

There are two *Clematis alpina* in the jewel garden, one in the spring garden
and a *Clematis macropetala* in the walled garden. All grow up tripods, except
the one in the spring garden that escaped into a hawthorn a few years back.
Macropetala is my favourite, the violet sharded sepals like a child's drawing of
stars in a brilliant sky. And you have to really look, pay attention. It is only there
for two weeks at the most and then gone for another year.

Because we started with a bare field every choice has been our own, but
our style and range of plants has hardly changed in the last twenty years.
Looking back over old garden notebooks there are pages of plant lists that
we still consistently use. Although we have visited hundreds of gardens
together, read millions of words and scoured countless pictures we seem
to end up with the same limited palette. The truth is that I don't want
endless choice. I want to limit the options otherwise it becomes too
overwhelming and I can't make a decision. I try to keep stripping the
components of the garden back rather than always adding to them. It
seems to me that the ideal is to have exactly and only the plants you want.

The swallows arrive sometime at the end of April, exhausted, all the way from Africa. One of my regrets about buying the barns and making them into human spaces is that we have deprived the swallows of some nesting sites. But we still have three or four pairs in our buildings, occasionally swooping in through the front door, doing a turn in the house and out again. I associate all summer with their presence, carving great arcs of sky above the garden.

The frost watches. We have never fooled it yet. The temptation to plant out tender annuals and to put out the pots of agapanthus and brugmansia in the first few weeks of May is always very great, but never worth the risk. We have had frost on 9th June before now so we wait with the cold frames crammed and the standing-out area jostling with flowers outgrowing their pots. The lesson, of course, is that it is better to be a little late with seed sowing than a little early. From the vantage point of early May autumn seems a long way away, but a couple of weeks' delay in spring can extend the flowering season for a month or more in September and October. That's the theory. In practice it takes discipline.

Apple blossom is much less blossomy than pear or plum. Perhaps the shades of pink do not have the impact of white blossom. No matter. The orchard in the first week of May is drenched with flower.

A mown path in the growing grass of the orchard can be as beautiful as a border packed with flowers. Just the different textures of green in May are more than enough.

I like the way that at this time of year the garden fills its spaces on its own. The poppies grow inches every day and marigolds seed everywhere. The garden becomes almost unbearably beautiful. Every second is precious. But time goes so fast and I can hardly breathe with the pace and excitement of it. I keep thinking, this is it. This is the moment.

Sometime around the beginning of the second week of May the tulips outstay their welcome. It is not that they are not good – just not as good as they were. There is a falling off. I want them to walk off stage at the peak of their performance. Anyway, there are other things in the wings.

The May blossom arrives uncannily near 11th May – the old May Day before the introduction of the Georgian calendar added eleven days in 1752. The combination of cow parsley and hawthorn blossom by the hundreds of mile is one of the glories of the world. Much hawthorn hedgerow has been grubbed out over the last fifty years, but, here in the West of England, much remains. To flower it must remain uncut from midsummer at the latest, so the more overgrown and unreachable the hedge the better the display. We have two hawthorns in the garden that were here when we came and our boundary is ringed with them – the outgrown ghosts of a laid hedge.

In the spring garden the combination of hawthorn, cow parsley, Solomon's seal, the species roses *R. hugonis* and *R.* 'Cantabrigiensis', forget-me-nots, euphorbias, aquilegias and the two tulips 'White Triumphator' and 'West Point' are as good as anything in the garden can ever be.

In May the damp garden is almost entirely green other than the flower tiers of *Viburnum plicatum* 'Mariesii' and the pink quince blossom. But the ligularias, hostas and regal fern *Osmunda regalis* are green on green, all edged with a high hedge of green hornbeam. It is like diving into a cool green pool.

The yew cones in the front and the box balls in the hopkiln yard develop just enough new growth to infuse them with new colour. Actually the clipped box pebbles only grow a little, then stop until midsummer, because they are infested with box psyllid – an aphid that sucks the sap and restricts the vigour. This suits me fine as it seems to do little long-term harm and means only clipping once, in August.

The beech woods and hazel coppices of our childhoods were a-shimmer with bluebells in May. We both wanted that memory here so

planted the native *Hyacinthoides non-scripta* in the spring garden. But a friend, hearing that we had planted the bulbs, told us we were barmy. Bluebells and borders don't mix, as the bluebells will ultimately take over. So we moved them to the coppice where they are gradually spreading, competing with the nettles that we keep meaning to dig out every winter.

––––––––––

Chelsea Flower Show always takes place sometime in the last two weeks in May. For five of the past seven years I have spent all week there, as part of the team covering it for both Channel 4 and the BBC. Chelsea is lovely to visit for a day, but to miss our garden at this time of year is a high price to pay. Surrounded by every species of plant that can be grown, each to the highest standard in the world, I pine for cow parsley and hawthorn.

The new green foliage of May is as intense as any emerald. Looking across the box pebbles in the hopkiln yard to the herb garden.

I started going to Chelsea in the early Eighties, long before Montagu had any professional connection with it. He would often refuse to come with me as he hated crowds (still does) and preferred to spend the precious May day in the garden. I remember Beth Chatto's stand had naturalistic planting and was completely unlike anything else there. I loved it and her style has remained a source of inspiration. I still go every year and am impressed by so many of the genuine nurserymen and -women who show there. But I miss the heady scent of the old canvas marquee first thing in the morning.

Recently though I was shocked by bales of Irish peat moss being used to titivate the show gardens and stands, at a time when the RHS as a body is trying to reduce the amount of peat used in horticulture. Even some show gardens that are trying to be as naturalistic as possible use peat, thereby helping to destroy one of the habitats they are seeking to portray. It seems that all integrity is thrown to the wind in pursuit of a gold medal. The chemical regimes needed to provide the flowers to create many

Left, the leaves of the martagon lily rise up through *Allium* 'Purple Sensation', oriental poppy and *Knautia macedonica*.

Right, grasses with a mown path, hawthorn hedges, field maples and a hammock. More would be too much.

The translucent
ruby shark-fin
thorns of
*Rosa sericea
pteracantha.*
If left unpruned
it is one of the
first roses, with
white flowers
in early May.

Chelsea show gardens are so artificial that in nature no wildflowers would grow anywhere near them. It is not credible.

I also think it a pity that so many plants are artificially held back or brought on just to be at their best for Chelsea, regardless of their natural flowering time. It would be a real and inspiring challenge for people only to show plants that are in season.

Chelsea week is always when the species roses are at their best and the other shrub roses are emerging. I love the unfussy simplicity allied to a spare toughness that is typical of species roses. The primrose-like flowers of R. *hugonis* and R. 'Cantabrigiensis' in the spring garden are followed in the jewel garden by blood red R. *moyesii* and R. *sericea pteracantha*, which we grow not for its flowers but for the crimson, fin-like thorns it carries.

I constantly take photographs of this garden and sometimes sit late into the night, out of season, looking back through them. Now, at the end of the year, I am looking back at 24th May.

Odd how some tulips stay for ages. The 'White Triumphator' in the lime walk are still – just – petalled. Likewise 'Queen of Night'. I've got them there on the screen in front of me. Digital memory. And on the same day – the day before I went to Chelsea for a week – the laburnum is dripping gold.

OVERLEAF
By mid-May
the jewel
garden is filling
daily. Here
the accidental
but managed
combination
of self-sown
red orache,
bronze fennel
and *Euphorbia
palustris*
'Zauberflöte'
with aquilegias
and thalictrum
catch the
morning light.

On that day, under the laburnum and against the chalky green of the cardoons, the first 'Purple Sensation' alliums are flowering and a single 'Beauty of Livermere' poppy has opened. The orange bracts of *Euphorbia griffithii* 'Fireglow' carry on where the orange parrot tulips are just leaving off. The orache and the chocolate purple leaves of *Lysimachia ciliata* 'Firecracker' are challenging the green of the jewel garden. The spring garden, such a primped and polite place between February and the beginning of May, has become wonderfully chaotic with flowers. Ah, you should have seen it. You should have been there.

Oriental
poppies in the
jewel garden.

Adam's birthday, Whitsun and Hay Literary Festival all come together in the same week as a big celebration at the end of May. The bright hopefulness of spring is replaced by a full and gleaming maturity.

This is when we want to show off the garden and share it with as many friends as possible. We have little time for a social life and because we live in an isolated part of the country, visitors are few and far between. But when people do come here we love to make an effort and have meals that last for hours sitting round a big trestle table in the walled garden.

The light changes. In April and May it is crystalline and seems to get inside the tissue of leaves and petals. By the end of May the sunshine washes over and around everything. And there is just more of it; bright light from four in the morning until late at night.

The evenings between Whitsun and midsummer – 24th June – are the best of the year. It does not begin to get dark until about 9.30 pm and on a clear day it is still light enough to work outside at 10 pm. This transforms our lives. It means that it is possible to spend a full day at work and still have two or three hours outside in the garden. The messiest day is made redeemable. The evening meal moves later and later with the light until by June we are not eating till after ten.

OVERLEAF
We let the herb
garden flower
for a month in
early summer,
but otherwise
it is a green
place set off by
the red brick
of the house.

One of the good weed trees in this garden is elder. We have never planted it but encourage it to grow in the boundary hedge. In the first couple of weeks of June it is covered in white frothy heads of flower. These only last ten days or so and suddenly brown and disappear but they are as much a marker of the year as cow parsley or holly berries. I pick them to make elderflower cordial. Every year I make more than before, but every year there is never enough.

All tender plants, edible and floral, can be planted out after Whitsun. Frost after this date can and does happen but it is freakish. The daytime temperature is pretty irrelevant as long as it stays above about 16 degrees centigrade. But if the nights stay warm then everything will steadily grow. However it is not at all unusual for June to have a week or two that are cold and miserable and all the tender plants sit looking desperately uncomfortable. Welcome to a British summer.

There is floral welcome enough. At the beginning of June the alliums are at their best, with *A. hollandicum* 'Purple Sensation' dominating the jewel garden and long walk and *A. cristophii* and *A. schubertii* bowling along in the walled garden. Cristophii always reminds me of a toy the children had when they were babies, a woven willow ball with a bell inside, and schubertii is a frozen explosion of a flower. One year we planted *A. giganteum* all the way down the long walk, and the vast melon-sized purple balls of flower on five-foot stems looked astonishing, but we left the bulbs in the ground and all but a handful rotted off over winter.

The long walk is tricky but important. It is a forty-yards-long, four-yards-wide passageway, leading out into the landscape, that gives a breathing space between the vegetable garden and the jewel garden, both of which are intense, busy spaces. These proportions were not artfully arrived at – they just sort of felt right. The walls of this outdoor corridor are about twelve feet high, as are all the hedges and pleached limes in this part of the garden, so the cross section is a square. A rule of design I try and follow is that all proportions should be based around the human body, and this seems to be a comfortable space.

The long walk is a little too enclosed for sun-loving plants to thrive and the soil is heavy and inclined to be damp so the ligularias and hostas would probably be happy there, but it is a little too ribbon-like to have anything but very simple, repetitive planting. We have experimented with cardoons flanking the whole length, which was wonderful until midsummer, after which all the flower stems leaned in an etiolated – and dangerously spiky – fashion towards the middle.

PREVIOUS PAGES *Left*, the flower head of *Allium cristophii* in the walled garden is just opening. Behind it is *Nepeta faassenii*. *Right*, the long walk. The under-planting is changed two or three times a year. Here *Allium hollandicum* 'Purple Sensation' is just opening.

I never tire of looking down the long walk because it frames the view to the river. There is always something beyond the garden that draws your eye, like a swan, a heron or even just a cow staring back. But the view from the other end looking back up to our barns is a mess. Perhaps I should design a gate or door to close it off.

We now have 'Handsworthiensis' box planted regularly down each side, being trained to become irregular pebble shapes. We grow wallflowers packed between them (Blood Red at the moment but our minds remain open from year to year) on a scale that fills the air with a honeyed scent, so for a few weeks it becomes a tunnel of rich red fragrance that we dip in and out of as we go about the garden. They are under-planted with tulips ('Abu Hassan', 'Queen of Sheba' and 'Flaming Parrot' – all of which are also in the jewel garden so we have a cunning colour link), which are then all lifted along with the wallflowers and replaced with . . . well, it varies. One year sweet peas looked great – twenty wigwams on either side covered in flower and perfume – but when we cleared them in October the space looked so much better.

The wallflowers look good because of their massed effect – they are really just park bedding. When they are over and the tulips have finished their flowering, which will be mid-May, we dig the whole lot up, compost the wallflowers, store the tulip bulbs and continue the bedding theme with dahlias, limiting the colours to shades of red and orange. All this is labour-intensive but we think the effect justifies the time and effort.

In the jewel garden the oriental poppies take on the June shift. They have a herbaceous softness that has none of the tulips' precision or restraint. Oriental poppies are dressed in ball gowns and frilly, furry ones at that. We have 'Beauty of Livermere', which is the tallest and a rich, deep scarlet, 'Allegro', which is

OVERLEAF
Left, oriental poppy; *right*, opium poppy.

shorter and almost orange with a deep alizarin centre, and 'Patty's Plum', which is very slow to establish and is either a dirty browny pink or a fascinating shade of mauve – I am undecided.

PREVIOUS PAGES
Opium poppy
seed heads.

We grew 'Pizzicato' from seed intended for the jewel garden. This has mixed flowers, something that we rather fastidiously avoid in general, but the good colours – which in jewel garden terms means the deep, rich ones – are very good and we dig up the pinks and whites that inevitably appear and move them to the walled garden. The 'Pizzicato' poppies have spread vigorously and seed themselves so are difficult to control as you never know what colour will emerge. But we like their gaudy, fairground colours and they make fantastic cut flowers.

Opium poppies follow on in mid-June as the oriental poppies go over. Our original seeds were given to us by a fashion photographer for our London garden and we have collected seed from them every year since. The silvery leaves appear in spring between the tulips and the temptation is to leave them there. But thinning makes the plants grow stronger and their shimmery flowers can grow up to eye level. They only last for a day but this doesn't matter as every morning there are new flowers to see and you can never predict exactly how they will look. In just a few days I watch the progress of the bud, drooping from its stem, getting bigger and fatter until, just before it flowers it straightens and the bud bursts from its papery skin. All our original varieties have interbred so that the colours are a patchwork and not necessarily suitable for the jewel garden but the seed heads are dramatic and some are as large as golf balls. The birds peck through them to get at the seeds in autumn, leaving a lacy skeleton.

I wish we had more irises. We have the tall, china-blue *Iris sibirica* and the short, intensely deep, almost black *I. chrysographes*, both in the jewel garden.

We planted the stripy leaves and mauve flowers of *I. pallida* 'Argentea Variegata' in the walled garden but it has never thrived. But why do we not have the browns and gingers, rust and burgundy colours of irises that would look so good in the June jewel garden? It is odd how the absences in a garden can become institutionalised. Maybe it is just us.

For a long time we didn't have the foxtail lily, eremurus, which is another June gem, and for ages it was in the same longed-for category. It is a grassland plant, surviving by being unpalatable to grazing cattle and going dormant in the baking South African summer. So our lush Herefordshire borders are about as far from its habitat as they could be. But it has made itself perfectly at home here. We have a few pure white *himalaicus* in the walled garden and I planted dozens of orange 'Cleopatra' in the jewel garden a year ago. Eremurus needs good drainage, which meant digging out a bucket of soil for each one and replacing it with a mixture of leaf mould and sharp sand so that the fleshy, spidery roots need never sit in the damp. I like eremurus best in the early morning when the sun rises over the top of the yew hedge that encloses the walled garden and the spires catch light, becoming gloriously incandescent.

These torches of flower only last for about twenty minutes over perhaps a week around midsummer when they are in full rig and the sun hits just that point. You need a cloudless morning and a deliberate, perfectly timed visit to catch them. Get busy or get lazy and you'll miss it. But I create these assignations all the time with this garden, brief, breathtaking moments that I long for all year.

In mid-December I'm looking at pictures I took in the early evening of 14th June last year. From here, as far away from June as I could be, it is a dreamtime. Seeing flowers float in clouds through the borders is the same lurch as seeing someone you love across a crowded room. The litany of plants sing from the badly focused pictures: a blizzard of crambe; white foxgloves leaning

Eremurus in the walled garden with the kind of planting jumble, poised on the brink of chaos, that we love.

out of the shade of the lime walk above a froth of alchemilla; roses with names like French romantic novels – Chapeau de Napoléon, cuisse de nymphe, 'Souvenir du Docteur Jamain', 'Charles de Mills'; *Knautia macedonica* dotted over alliums, over iris, over marguerites; and a fuzz of fennel foliage. This didn't just happen. Sarah and I made it. For a moment I feel like an evangelical cheerleader. Feel *good* about yourselves! Look what you have made!

What amazes me most is the maturity of it all. Because it has grown from an empty field and because I have busied so much, head down, on always to the next thing, I had not really noticed how much it has grown up. Somehow, after ten years, it has reached a kind of adulthood. For years it has been something that Sarah and I have nurtured and helped along but now the relationship has changed. Someone else could maintain it more or less as it is.

We are always losing labels. Usually this does not matter as we can look names up or check through an old plant order. But it can result in hours hunting through books. This is the case with many of our clematis. We have at least half a dozen that are not identified. I can't say I care very much.

Clematis has always seemed to me to be such good value, and it is not just a climber with lovely flowers but an essential structural element in the jewel garden. Almost all our clematis grow on wigwams made from bean sticks providing instant height in a border, but they have to be replaced every two or three years. This is no problem with the late-flowering clematis, such as any of the viticellas or Jackmaniis, as they have to be pruned right down to the base every spring, so it is easy to remove the rotten sticks and put in new. But the alpinas are more of a fiddle and their top growth has to be carefully disentangled and laid to one side before being fixed back to the new support. This is best done around the middle of May, immediately after flowering.

OVERLEAF
Two yardsticks of colour in the jewel garden. *Left, Anchusa azurea* 'Loddon Royalist'; *right, Rosa moyesii* 'Geranium'.

Most of our clematis, like 'Gipsy Queen' or 'Perle d'Azur', run along the colour spectrum from blue to deep purple but 'Niobe' is a velvety burgundy and the double flowers of the peerless *C. viticella* 'Purpurea Plena Elegans' are maroon. But that comes later in the summer. By mid-June the huge violet flowers of 'The President' are at their best and 'Honora' is flowering along with the only rose in the jewel garden, 'Scharlachglut'.

On Valentine's Day 1996 Sarah gave me a dozen bushes of this exceptionally spiky, vigorous shrub rose, which has brilliant crimson, almost magenta flowers that fade in sunlight to a cherry pink. Pruning it is one of the worst jobs of the year – invariably a thorn gets embedded in my scalp and nothing short of a crash helmet will protect against this, but it is beautiful in flower and in spirit.

Clematis are an important element of the jewel garden. Here 'Hildora' is in flower and 'Gipsy Queen' is just about to break bud behind me.

The delphiniums grow against a backdrop of a weeping silver pear and cardoon; the silvery green of both accentuates the blue towers of flower. They are not really blue, of course – in the garden almost nothing is when you look closely. Almost all garden blues are versions of violet. There are exceptions that prove this rule like meconopsis or *Anchusa azurea* 'Loddon Royalist' but to insist on the distinction would be pedantry. We want delphiniums to be blue, so blue they become. We have two types, Black Knight, which is a dark indigo with a black eye that makes the whole flower verge into navy, and King Arthur, which is inky blue with a white eye – the combined effect merges into a paler blue.

Baptisia australis has lovely pea-like indigo flowers set against pale foliage, which the magenta geranium 'Ann Folkard' peaks through. The baptisia grew for three years without being remotely convincing but has recently come good in a spectacular way, and, unlike delphiniums, it is completely slug-proof.

Delphiniums, like harsh grass on bare knees or cups of tea in the sunshine, are a measure of summer from my childhood – they grew well on the chalk of Hampshire. Now that I think about it, I suppose they were a rare glimpse of home in June – which between the ages of seven and 17 I saw for at

most two days over half-term weekend. By the time term ended around the middle of July the delphiniums were past their best and cut back. So I leave ours too long, draining the last dregs of blue and liberty from them. I should be more ruthless and cut them back once they start to go over so that they have time to flower again in late summer.

Another tall spire that we leave to its dregs is the foxglove. We have white ones all the way down the lime walk. By the beginning of July they are all but over, leaning over the path in a drunken topple. The idea, of course, that something is 'over' derives from a kind of horticultural gentility where nothing must be seen to be less than at its best, as though the garden must always be in its best bib and tucker for the public gaze. But we rather like the louche unravelling of plants as they go from perfect flowers to seediness.

The days between 21st and 24th June are the summit of the year. England, in the country, in a garden, at midsummer, is as good as it will ever be. I would like to celebrate this with bacchanalian feasting, wine and music, but all too often these days slip by, passing through the net of business, bad weather and inattention. As a public gardener this is my busiest time of year. When I do get outside – usually between 8 and 10 pm – it is to try and get done as much as light and weariness will allow. This is not good gardening. Too much bustling satisfies a sense of self, but the easy joy and poetry is trampled if you are not careful. And if you cannot reach the joy and poetry at midsummer then they will remain unattainable.

The jewel garden runs down to water meadows that are flooded in winter, but in summer cattle grow fat on the rich grass.

The garden undergoes a gradual change throughout June, reaching a peak that is unsustainable. Things fall apart. The burnished virility of June becomes shaggy and plants that carelessly spilled out of the borders begin to flop.

This is not unattractive. July arrives with a lived-in, worldly air that is something of a relief after all the bustling vigour of spring and early summer. My horticultural response is to cut back and clear the fading flowers of early summer, such as oriental poppies, geraniums or catmint, before things get too loose. This then creates space for more planting and lets in light and air. But Sarah is always more reluctant to lose the careless looseness that accompanies the turn from early to high summer.

In order to make way for new planting to grow and also the regeneration of things like geraniums, oriental poppies and delphiniums I know that there has to be some ruthless cutting back. But it always looks horrible for a couple of weeks.

We have never really got the succession right. One of the things I admire most in gardens open to the public is the way that they manage to maintain a display week in, week out. Here we tend to focus on different areas at different times of year. By July the spring garden, which is the centre of attention between January and May, is unvisited and ignored. The walled garden does little before May and starts to get boring by August. The damp garden performs from May to September with its peak in July. The jewel garden, however, carries on with all sails unfurled from late April to November – but the only time that all the different gardens work together is during the last two weeks of May.

OVERLEAF
A frozen dance of bupleurum, *Rubus cockburnianus* 'Goldenvale', *Knautia macedonica* and *Euphorbia palustris*.

Around the beginning of July there is a real sense of something ending. For many years perhaps that was something to do with my birthday on the 8th.

Two gardening styles – Sarah considering things, Montagu looking like he needs a cup of tea.

But I now realise that subconsciously I am reacting to the days getting shorter. The slide down to the low point of the year has begun even though summer is only just getting into its stride. The result is confusion and regret that takes a while to overcome.

Montagu is always exhausted and very difficult around the time of his birthday. It is a bad time of year for him. From spring he has worked so hard – almost manically – filming, writing, gardening every daylight hour, that by July he is exhausted and very vulnerable. His usual carapace is worn too thin. He needs time at home and as few demands upon him as possible. Unfortunately it is the time of year when his work schedule is most pressurised and demanding. It is a problem but we try and manage it. Probably no one else notices.

The biggest job in July is to cut the hedges. This takes about three weeks from start to finish, of which half is spent clearing up the mess. Put like that it sounds an appalling chore but I like it. Apart from anything else it makes a dramatic difference. The hedges in this garden are much more than just a backdrop to flowers. They define and shape the spaces.

The hedge cutting is genuinely hard work, involving holding a heavy, noisy petrol-driven cutter at awkward heights and angles for long periods in hot sunshine. Only the box hedges can be cut from the ground. All the hornbeam, field maple and hawthorn hedges require the constant assembling and moving of scaffolding, steps or mobile platforms. It is a kerfuffle. In amongst the muscular palaver and sweat there is also a degree of skill. Cut too much and you ruin it for months. Cut too little and you lose the edge. Do the whole garden right and the visual effect lasts right through till autumn.

One of the bonuses of hedge cutting is that I get to see the garden from on high. Since I am the only person who is not bothered by heights, the topping of the hedges is always down to me.

I absolutely hate the sound of machines in the garden. Mowers, Rotovators, hedge cutters are all a kind of torture. I want *peace*.

But there are some sounds that I do love to hear. By late July the young buzzards mew and noisily complain in the fields by the river as their parents leave them to learn how to hunt. A quiet garden allows the year to be measured by these sounds.

By the middle of July a new shift of flowers takes over. *Crocosmia* 'Lucifer' is at its best and adds an intensity of red that has been absent since the oriental poppies finished. The flowers seem to land on their curving stems like a flock of outrageous butterflies, quite separate from the sheath of leaves that provides their backdrop. Over the past twenty years or so 'Lucifer' has not only become triumphantly popular but has introduced the idea of glamour into all crocosmias. It is one of those plants that has a ripple effect – you can almost see the rays of influence emanating from them, setting the tone for the whole garden.

Crocosmia
'Lucifer' burns
a brilliant
crimson flame
in high
summer.

The sweet peas and clematis are rampant with flower and, compared to the crocosmia, get taken for granted, although few other plants provide such a mass of flowers over such a long period without losing their freshness.

In the damp garden the ligularias have their day. Until 2000 the ligularias were all in the jewel garden, where they looked superb. On a good day. But they respond dramatically to drying out, flopping as though struck with some terrible blight. Like all moisture-loving plants, this effect can be delayed by planting them in shade but in the jewel borders they were exposed to full sunshine all day long. So I dug them up and moved them to become the heart of a new garden in an area that is the first to flood and the last to dry out. The high hornbeam hedges shade it from the hottest sun and we planted hostas, royal ferns, primulas, *Euphorbia palustris* and *Lysimachia ciliata* 'Firecracker'.

One of the problems of the damp garden is that every year the floods bring in thousands of weed seeds, so you need a thug to combat them. Lysimachia does that job very well. It looks good too. The chocolate leaves with their tiny yellow flowers are handsome and dramatic and if it spreads too much then we just dig it up by the barrow-load and add it to the compost heap. There are some plants that you should not be precious about.

The lysimachia flowers chime with the prevailing yellowness of the ligularias, which start flowering in July and for about two weeks create a xanthic fanfare from the chrome yellow of 'Desdemona' through to the egg yolk orange of 'Othello'. *Ligularia* 'The Rocket' and *L. przewalskii* shoot up on spires, the stems of the latter as black as the canes of the bamboo *Phyllostachys nigra* that grows in the jewel garden.

OVERLEAF
The damp
garden in July.
*Ligularia
przewalskii* and
L. 'The Rocket'
with royal
ferns, *Osmunda
regalis*, at their
base. All self-
sow freely and
love the wet
ground in
this corner of
the garden.

We have masses of acanthus in the garden, especially *Acanthus spinosus*. Their flower spikes are at their best at this time of year but their profusion is entirely down to a clerical error. I ordered four from a catalogue but forty were delivered. I realise that most people would have sent the excess back

but I didn't double-check the order until too late. So we planted the full forty. The flower spikes make fantastic cut flowers but they are like barbed wire and inevitably scratch you as you cut them.

Moving plants is our weakness. We rearrange them until it feels right and the plant is happy. But there are always failures. Penstemons, campanulas and lobelias have never done well for us despite moving them round to find the ideal spot. We now know what grows well here and increasingly I feel that straining to grow a plant that does not feel at home in this garden is a waste of time.

The Madonna lilies in the walled garden have, after a few years settling in, become reliably sumptuous, but only three of the fifty martagon lilies we planted in the jewel garden survived. Why? These three are stunning – although if we were more ruthless we would move them because they are too pink for those borders.

Dahlia 'Bishop of Llandaff'. We try and dead-head soon after this phase, before the petals fade.

The dahlia 'Bishop of Llandaff' is a bright red rock to which the jewel garden is tethered in late summer. I couldn't care less that this particular dahlia is now ubiquitous in all well-bred gardens. It does a wonderful job for us, but there are others that would work as well, if in a different way. We must grow more dahlias. Many more dahlias. The secret of dahlias is to dead-head all the time. I always carry secateurs with me and every time I walk through the jewel garden – which is between four and twenty times a day – I snip the flowers as soon as the edges of the petals start to fade and the centres become bright yellow. Inevitably masses slip through this brutal net but it does keep the colours intense and also means that they flower right into autumn. Same for sweet peas, cosmos, the only floribunda rose in the garden, heleniums, brugmansias, tithonias. Snip away and they will keep coming back for more.

By August the orache is over six feet tall, and heavy with deep plum-coloured seed. This spinach is a colour-crop, filling the garden with burgundy,

Left to right,
Helenium
'Marmalade',
sunflower
'Velvet Queen'
and *Crocosmia*
× *crocosmiiflora*
'Emily
McKenzie'.

plum, purple and then, as it fades in autumn, tawny ochre. Sometimes we take the extent of this purple foil for granted, but it is probably the single dominating plant of the jewel garden, giving a depth and intensity to the flower colours that green foliage would not provide.

I love the rich oranges and browns of late summer. Sunflowers like 'Velvet Queen', *Crocosmia* × *crocosmiiflora* 'Emily McKenzie', heleniums 'Marmalade' and 'Moerheim Beauty', *Tithonia rotundifolia* 'Torch', leonotis, marigolds, nasturtiums – all look particularly good in the evening sun which, for about three weeks in late August and early September, falls low enough to strike against these orange flowers and yet strong enough to blaze.

OVERLEAF
Left, a snail's-eye
view of golden
hop; *right,* the
dried heads of
Allium cristophii
and *Allium*
aflatunense
ready to be
stored for winter
arrangements.

In the first week of September, the summer holidays are over and a new year begins. All change. New year, new form, new school, new season. The garden often seems unaware of this, carrying on its summer ways. But it is on borrowed time.

Somehow it is easy to treat September as an extension to August or a prelude to October, but it is as distinctive a month as any, and has its own quality of light that is more fragile than the glare of summer or the rich honey slant of autumn. It is this light that you easily forget.

I really love September because the pressure is off. There is nothing that you can do to alter the way things are. It is a time simply to enjoy the garden as it is. One of the great advantages of our heavy wet soil is that most years the borders look good right into September and do not have that tired, August slump that we always had to contend with in London.

The tobacco plants, *Nicotiana sylvestris*, are at their best in the little box-edged borders just outside the hall door. They have white Rastafarian dreadlocks of flower and great sticky leaves that, by late summer, are lushly tropical. Last year Tommy spent a day drying them in a smoker made of cast-off bricks and stone, then rolling them into cigarettes. They smelt of cigars but tasted of nothing. The best of times.

Even though it is not technically a jewel colour, orange is a vital part of the jewel garden. It has an immediate effect on me, acting like sunlight, instantly making me feel energised. There is a lot of orange in the borders in spring with tulips, the eremurus 'Cleopatra' and the orange imperial fritillaries, but after this orange does not appear much until late summer and early autumn, when it reappears with a vengeance. The flower borders

By September the harvest is in and the artichokes are going to seed faster than we can eat them.

OVERLEAF Two of our favourite late-summer tender annuals, *Tithonia rotundifolia, left,* and *Leonotis leonurus, right.* Both flower right through to the first frosts.

continue to be dominated by sunflowers, heleniums, tithonia, leonotis, marigolds and nasturtiums – although the latter are the first to be blasted by frost. Even this is not enough. Although I am resisting it, Montagu wants to grow orange cannas, orange ginger, orange kniphofias and orange dahlias. My love of orange will certainly be tested to the full.

The clipped box balls take on a new light and become emerald cabochons in the evening sun. For three or four weeks the sun seems invariably to break through any cloud in the early evening and the whole of the back of the garden catches this intense, low glow. At the beginning of September, this is between 6.30 and 8. By the end of the month it is 5 to 7. The substance of the day is slipping away.

As a young boy I can still remember remaining bombed-out ruins from the Second World War, all overgrown with buddleias. Now they flank every loose, limy railway siding in the country and I struggle a little to think of them as precious, radiant flowers, but this is what they become at the back end of summer. We have 'Black Knight' and 'Royal Red', the latter treading the imperial ground where red and purple meet.

The butterflies flutter around them. Red admirals, peacocks, painted ladies, commas, tortoiseshells, brimstones, orange-tips and skippers all queue for landing space. This is one of the unexpected harvests of the jewel garden – so many flowers all grown together brings in flocks of butterflies and birds – greedy for nectar and seeds. Blackbirds and thrushes are especially numerous and spread mulch all over the paths as they scratch around for worms.

Verbena bonariensis is one of the key late-summer plants in the jewel garden. It comes from wet, open fields in South America and mixes well with grasses.

In fact it mixes well with almost anything, its tall fluted stems rising between its neighbours without ever intruding or being intruded upon. The butterflies love them, treating each tiny flower as a nectar mini-bar. Unfortunately it is unreliable, seeding itself all over the place some years, cropping up especially in the uncultivated edges of the vegetable garden, then disappearing completely the next. It is not fully hardy, although sometimes survives winter to emerge in a very bedraggled state.

September is usually our driest month. The soil holds water well but a long dry summer uses up all the reserves. We also often get light frosts at the end of September, around the autumn equinox, coming out of bright, hot days. These tend to damage the tender vegetables and herbs more than flowers like dahlias or cosmos, which can survive three or four degrees of frost. But it is an intimation of winter.

I always take a batch of at least a hundred box cuttings in September or early October, building up stock to use for edging borders. Over the years I have tried lots of ways of doing this but I find that sticking them straight into a sheltered bed in the vegetable garden, with extra grit dug in to improve drainage, is as successful a method as any. They stay there for a year, by which time they have roots but no top growth, are moved to the nursery bed for another two years and then planted out into their final position. Within five years they make a solid hedge and the best winter structure that any garden can have.

OVERLEAF
In autumn the grasses come to dominate the jewel garden. *Miscanthus* 'Purpurascens', *left*, and *Miscanthus sinensis* 'Variegatus', *right*, both become soaked in rich colour.

This is harvest time. There are barrow-loads of fruit, herbs and vegetables to be prepared for keeping over winter. For weeks I hardly do any gardening at all other than pick big bunches of flowers for the house.

The swallows line up on the telephone wire that loops across the front garden, chattering and jostling for space. For years we have talked of burying it, but I think we would miss the swallows more than we would appreciate the tidier air.

When not perching they feed frantically, fattening up for their journey. Then one day they are not there and the garden is emptier and sadder for it.

And I get sadder at this time too. It cannot be helped, but I always forget how powerfully I am affected. However, for a week or so I really enjoy the dark curtailing my evenings. It is a treat to finish work outside around seven, come in, have a bath and luxuriate in the enforced leisure. But only for a week or so.

October seems to be getting drier and drier. Sustained periods of dry weather mean going outside without putting on boots. Gardening in ordinary shoes – that is the real measure of drought in this garden. A dry autumn holds the leaves on the trees and hedges. They thin rather than fall. Horizontal light filters through where a month or so before there was deep shade.

> One of the flowers that looks at its best in the last warm days of autumn is chocolate cosmos. The dark maroon petals never seem to lose their intensity and continue to be produced up until the first really cold weather. And of course the children have always been fascinated by a flower that smells of chocolate.

By October colour leaches out of the garden. Only highlights of red, blue or yellow remain. *Knautia macedonica* will go on flowering well into autumn but fewer and fewer flowers replace those that go to seed and the weight of wiry stems falls upon itself, literally squashing anything growing in its lee. But cutting back at this stage is admitting defeat. This is all there is. There is nothing more to come. So we cling to these few fragile flowers.

The orache loses all the colour from its leaves and the stems fade to pink whilst the heads carry tens of thousands of flat seeds like dry, tawny frogspawn. These seeds fall at the slightest shake ensuring next year's crop. They are too heavy to be blown by the wind and the birds do not seem to take much interest in them, so they shower the base of each plant, keeping local.

We give the hedges another trim in October. This sends them crisply into winter and the edges remain right through till spring, defining the winter garden. I love the shapes that the newly cut hedges make for the week or so following this second trim. They still have their green leaves, recalling summer, but I know that it is all about to end.

Gradually there is an extraordinary yellowing of the leaves – especially the hornbeams and field maples – so that for three or four days in the second half of October the whole garden glows bright yellow. Then rain washes the leaves off their branches.

My diary tells the full autumn story in three days:

October 20th. Cold, lovely clear bits of blue sky. Leaves stunning.

October 21st. Wonderful cold, frosty morning. Minus five. Absolutely still. Leaves began clattering off the trees at 9am and fell like rain.

October 22nd. Grey, miserable, showery. Every fallen leaf has a smell. Figs are richly fragrant. Hornbeam woody. Hazel slightly sweet.

There is only one fact that matters at this time of year, which is that the light is slipping irretrievably away. Evening tightens like a noose and the mornings draw in the dark with astonishing speed. British Summer Time ends at 2 o'clock on the last Sunday morning of October. The clocks are all set an hour back. Our evenings outside, which have been getting shorter and shorter, now cease to exist.

Winter

Winter in this garden is like preparing a boat for a voyage. The evenings disappear and the weather usually turns grey and wet. It is hardly surprising that – to put it mildly – spirits drop. November and December are there to be endured.

There is some consolation. Bonfire night on the Saturday nearest to 5th November is a ritual we always observe – even if rain delays it for weeks. We have a bonfire on the go for most of the year, burning anything that will not recycle or compost, but we have a big clear-up in November to burn away the year. Chuck in a few wildly expensive fireworks and a Thermos of soup and a splendid time is guaranteed for all.

But then the garden slides inexorably downhill. Its texture becomes hostile. The grass is bobbled with worm casts and slimy unless frozen. Fallen leaves rattle into corners until it rains, when they make a wet, brown shell over plants, paths and pots. In fact leaves are a precious resource and we try and gather every last one, go over them with the mower to chop them up, and store them good and damp to rot down into leaf mould. But even the best leaf mould – which is so soft and crumbly and smells so earthily fresh – has to go through months of being no more than a pile of sodden leaves.

Any time spent outside at this time of year is completely weather-dependent. Unrelentingly grey days have a deadening effect on everybody. This is not like Montagu's depression – which has always really kicked in by early November – but just an instinctive response to the lack of light. It is a kind of hibernation.

We have always longed to go away at this time of year to the sun and let the garden look after itself for a few months. Unfortunately children, dogs and chickens cannot be left. So we stick it out.

OVERLEAF
The jewel garden in November after the big autumn tidy-up. This is done less for neatness than to clear space to move plants and plant bulbs.

By December it is dark at 4.30 pm and there are many days when the sun simply does not appear. Thick, grey cloud can hang over the garden for days on end, obscuring whatever the sun might be doing. Gloom is the only reasonable reaction. The last six weeks of the year are often very wet, turning the grass into a quagmire that can scarcely be walked on – let alone bear the weight of a barrow. This is why we have added as many hard paths to the garden as we have been able to afford. They are very expensive and slow to make but the only way of getting round the garden in a wet winter. Our rainfall is not particularly high – around 35 to 40 inches a year – but the ground remains wet for months on end in winter, relieved only by hard frost. Periodical flooding keeps the ground sodden.

The flooding changes everything. If we had known its extent then the layout of the garden would probably have been quite different but our first few years here were unusually dry. By the time that the flooding had resumed its usual pattern, the garden had been laid out and now it has become part of its character. The water rises astonishingly fast, pouring down from the Welsh mountains some twenty miles to the west. Once the river bursts its banks it spreads across hundreds of acres in a matter of minutes. Any stock has to be rounded up and taken off the fields fast by driving them down the roads. We have often watched stranded cattle diving into the river and swimming across to safety. But somehow the house feels secure on its raised platform. At its height the flood puts most of the spring garden under water, covers half the vegetable garden and all of the damp garden. It is a strange thing to look down and see snowdrops and hellebores beneath the surface.

In 2000, after a month of incessant rain, we had six weeks when our septic tank did not function, which meant no baths, washing up, washing machines or flushing loos. I finally had had enough of washing everything – including ourselves – in a yellow bucket and moved with the children into a hotel in Hereford. Montagu stayed behind as he rather enjoyed the discomfort, treating it like an extended camping trip.

The winter of 2000 was exceptionally wet right across the country. But often November is merely drab and the best we can expect is frost, which at least is dry.

15th November. Hoar frost overnight. I lay in bed too angry at the fact that I was awake to go back to sleep and too tired to get up – even though I remembered that I had left a rice pudding in the oven. The owls shrieked and hooted and snuffled. At one point, about half past three, the cattle started mooing very loudly. Why? I could hear nothing that might have provoked it. When I got up the freezing fog was rolling in through the window. Outside the back door the thermometer reads minus three. Frost is to November and December what sunshine is to May and June. It belongs to the season and yet it always arrives as a treat to be relished. After last year's deluge this autumn has been extraordinarily dry, with October the hottest on record. This is the bright face of global warning, the holiday in fine weather whilst the crops burn up a mile in from the sea. But we desperately need bursts of frost from November through to March. Frost kills the caterpillars and slugs, scours through the fungal diseases and infections in the soil and crevices of bark, washes the wind. It breaks down the soil, gives a few hours' hard ground so barrows can be wheeled and lawns are not sludgy. It is the organic gardener's firm ally.

And of course it is beautiful.

Went outside at first light and everything coated in white. The fennel heads extraordinary – worth keeping – in fact, worth growing them – just for this effect, even if it is only one day in the autumn. There seemed to be a lot of rustling of birds but in fact it was leaves constantly falling off the trees. Thousands upon thousands of leaves all falling at once although there was not a breath of wind. It was as though they had all lost their balance and were slipping off, bouncing on the branches, knocking more free as they passed, rocking and zigzagging down to the ground.

I must lift the dahlias, the gladioli and the cosmos before they get frosted underground. The tops are burnt and collapsed – as are the salvias. I brought half a dozen plants of Salvia elegans *in a week or two ago and have taken cuttings of* Salvia guaranitica, *both to see us into next year. I shall cut the frosted plants down to the ground and some might come through the cold to next spring.*

I photographed the garden at 9.30 and by 10 the frost was all gone, leaving skiddy dampness in its place. The limes dripped. Perhaps that is a mark of truly cold weather in Britain – when the frost remains even after the sun has got up.

If I take stock of what we have not done the list is long and shaming:

1. *No tulips planted, let alone narcissi, alliums, crocuses.*
2. *Nothing mulched.*
3. *Dahlias etc not dug up and stored.*
4. *Pond not begun.*
5. *Tomatoes in tunnel not cleared.*
6. *No real digging begun.*
7. *Broad beans not in the ground.*
8. *Spring garden not properly cleared.*
9. *No roses or other plants ordered – let alone planted.*
10. *Not one leaf collected yet.*

When the light goes at the beginning of November a great slab of will goes with it. So if things are not to hand when you are hands-free, they tend to be put off for another day. Winter seems long, but somehow time is very short between October and Christmas. There is much to do and one should be working on the assumption that the weather will always get worse.

I look out of the kitchen window and see flocks of fieldfares that have flown in from the north. As the last leaves fall you can see through the branches across the fields for the first time since April. It is astonishing how quickly the memory of summer disappears.

We first noticed ravens flying overhead about five years ago. They are now a fixture, often mobbed by crows. Working in the garden the sound of them makes one do a double take. It is extraordinarily deep – almost a grunt. We also see a peregrine flying overhead a few times a year. Each time is like a visitation. I have seen otters playing at the edge of the floods not fifty yards from our back door. For all our domesticity and the softness of the countryside, this is still a wild, unspoilt place.

Depending on the weather we cut back and clear the jewel garden borders throughout November. This is a big job and creates great windrows of dry stems and foliage. Initially it is too coarse for the compost heap, but we 'bash' it with the powerful rotary grass cutter, spreading it out in the orchard and mowing over it half a dozen times to chop it into small pieces before adding it to the compost, ready to return all that energy and goodness back to the soil.

This clearing is not a cull but is done slowly and carefully, with three or four passes over the month as we cling to every scrap of colour and life left in the borders. At the start of November there is still a lot left. The hornbeams surrounding the garden have turned an intense, glowing yellow and if we have had a mild autumn there will still be flowers of salvias, leonotis, *Verbena bonariensis*, dahlias, calendulas and aconitum. As we cut back more and more, bare soil appears, hidden since June. The spaces open out. The garden empties.

But the grasses come into their own with their ochres and russets and golds. The rich mounds of the pheasant grass are best of all at this time of year. They are hidden for much of the summer but the autumn clear-up lets them stand out for the rest of winter. Originally we dotted them around but

have now replanted them more formally as punctuation marks.

This rhythmic structure helps give the garden a shape it badly needs.

I like to leave as many tall things standing as winter ghosts for as long as they can support themselves. They also remind us how high things are in midsummer – which is easy to forget in the flat dreariness of midwinter.

We clear the borders to stop sodden vegetation rotting the plants they cover and so that we can get at the ground. There is always a lot of moving and splitting of plants to be done and when this is completed, bulbs to be added. Over the past three or four years we have planted over five thousand tulips and uncounted alliums, muscari, hyacinths and lilies. After years of bulbs making a rather weak contribution to the garden, they are now one of its strongest cards.

We leave the huge – and very spiky – stems of onopordum for as long as possible, although by Christmas most have tumbled in high winds.

Mass tulip planting has to be very organised. First we draw up a plan on cardboard that can be carried around outside. Then, using canes, we mark out the beds into one-yard squares. The same number of bulbs are allocated to each square and placed on the ground around the patchwork of perennials and shrubs so the final effect avoids being too regimented. Then each bulb is planted. Because we plant them only a few inches deep this does not take long. All books will recommend planting tulips at least four inches deep but many will be dug up and stored when we plant out tender annuals in June and the rest seem to do fine in our wet soil. The annual mulch effectively buries them a little deeper each year.

November is a counsel of perfection. The tulips do not always get planted before mid-January. It doesn't seem to matter.

By December there is not much to do in the garden. Everything is dormant. You can't even see where half the plants are. I barely go outside for days on end. But if it is a bright day or there is a hoar frost I am drawn outside.

On these days the garden has a monochrome austerity that I think looks good in the chilly sunlight. For this reason I like to leave all the fennel, grasses and cardoons and make the most of their bony winter structure.

But I really hate the cold. It makes my skin creep. I would much rather get cosy by the fire indoors.

21st December. The best things about midwinter:

• *The bamboo* Phyllostachys aureocaulis, *whose stems shine a brilliant lemon-curd yellow whenever there is the slightest hint of winter sun. We have moved our poor plant around three times now but it still remains astonishingly healthy and vibrant.*

• *Fennel heads – especially when lit by a coating of frost.*

• Melianthus major *in the walled garden. It survives the first hard frosts but around the turn of the year it rather gives up the ghost and browns to nothing. However it always reappears in spring.* Acanthus mollis 'Hollard's Gold' *behaves in exactly the same way.*

• Rubus cockburnianus. *A terrible thing to weed and plant around – it is, after all, just a spectacular bramble – but I can forgive it a lot for its milky purple sheen.*

• *Hips and haws. This is cheating really, because the haws do not last long into November. The birds gobble them up as soon as the weather turns cold. But the rose hips will remain right through to spring – 'Scharlachglut' are the biggest in the jewel garden, and* R. moyesii *'Geranium' are wonderful orange flagons.*

• *The rank tang of fox. Every morning I smell the fox that takes a short cut through the jewel garden at night, marking its way before passing on across the fields.*

The bloomy stems of *Rubus cockburnianus* look wonderful throughout winter, but it layers at every point it touches the ground, so has to be cut back hard in spring.

This garden stands naked from mid-November to March, revealing all its strengths and weaknesses of structure. It cannot be hidden by flowers. Increasingly I value green – any green – to temper the burden of brown and grey that weighs the garden down. Mown grass will not supply this. Here it is

the natives, box, yew and holly that do the job best, with a little assistance from Portuguese laurel, rosemary, wallflowers, *Acanthus mollis* and hellebores.

I wish I had taken more box cuttings ten years ago so that we could have hedged all our edges by now. It takes thousands of plants to do this but gradually we are accumulating the plants we need to give us a clipped framework around every bed. Winter is fuzzy and smudged enough as it is. Clean edges somehow add energy and purpose.

26th December. Incredibly bright, cold morning. Resolve to go outside, clean out chickens – which I have been putting off for weeks – and then do some pruning of limes. Read too long, make another cup of coffee, clear up kitchen, tidy big hall and it is time to prepare lunch. The only outside contact that I have had is to feed the chickens and check the greenhouse (nothing changes here for days. I check that there is nothing to check). Lunch is good (celeriac and chestnut soup) and I let it digest with a cup of very good Peruvian coffee. Adam puts on a video of the rugby and I watch it with him. It is now 3.30 and the weather has changed, becoming grey and raw, half-snow, half-rain. I feed the chickens again, empty the compost dustbin, dig up the celery (half-rotten and gone to seed – some good stuff amongst it but not worth the bother of extracting this ten per cent) and put it on the compost heap. My day outside is done. How many days mirror this?

Half the problem is that the garden is too small to contain my discontent. At The Hanburies the acres swallowed this up. I could go and fence a field, divert the stream or clear the wood and the sweep of space and action mitigated the fact that I was not doing half of what I had to do nor a tenth of what I wanted to do. Here it is more like not doing the washing up or tidying my desk. I find this smallness of domesticity depressing and boring.

The hips of *Rosa* 'Scharlachglut'. Good for the birds as well as colour-deprived humans.

The year turns on its heel on Boxing Day. From that moment everything gradually gets better. Christmas is celebrated with all its green-decked pagan

ceremony and we start all over again. For me it is a moment of profound relief. My mental and physical health always begin to recover. The urge to get out and tackle things starts to pull at my sleeve.

The garden responds. First to appear are snowdrops, pushing through the soil before Christmas like green knitting needles and then developing a pearl of bud before opening sometime in early January. I have gradually divided and spread our few stock plants along the path in the spring garden, moving them early every March whilst they are still 'in the green'. I have not an ounce of collector's acquisitiveness when it comes to snowdrops, despite the hundreds of different varieties that tempt galanthophiles. It is the *idea* of a snowdrop as much as any specific detail that captivates me. Most of all I like their longevity. They may only flower for a month in winter but I know that if they are left undisturbed, these snowdrops in our spring garden will gently multiply and flower for a month every year for hundreds of years, long after we are all forgotten.

Planting *Allium sphaerocephalon*. The bulbs are tiny and it is horribly fiddly work in cold weather.

The extraordinary thing is how little it takes to lift one's spirits. As soon as the snowdrops appear and the crowns of plants show signs of life, then all the possibilities of spring open out ahead. This is why we do it year after year. It can all seem so much effort and the good bits can be over all too quickly or we can be too busy or distracted to fully enjoy them, but the cycle renews itself with fresh intensity every year.

The winter honeysuckle, *Lonicera fragrantissima*, starts to flower around the shortest day, 21st December, and continues for another two months, leaves gradually replacing the delicate and astonishingly fragrant little white blooms.

When cut it not only looks as lovely as a bride but also fills a large room with a subtle and haunting scent, although it does drop all its ivory flowers like confetti.

Our flower-arranging technique is completely without fuss.
We simply rush out, cut whatever is looking good and pop it into a vase.
The spirit is always impulsive and the arrangement simple. We both do
a lot of this and it is an important part of our enjoyment of the garden.

As the snowdrops begin to fade the hellebores take over. Sometime between the beginning of November and the end of January I will remove all their leaves, probably in two or three passes, each time filling a barrow with their polished leathery foliage. The new leaves appear tentatively and are quickly overshadowed by the flowers on tall thick stems. Some early hellebores will flower in late January – there is one especially deep wine-coloured clump that is always weeks ahead of the others – but the majority do not really hit their stride until the end of February. In spring and summer you react to drifts and swirls of colour. But in January individual plants draw in all your attention.

The spring garden in January, bright with hope.

Any beginning or end in the gardening calendar is arbitrary. The year flows through the garden like a river that brings you back somewhere near to where you started. But by the end of February there is an atavistic, irresistible urge to be outside. Half an hour of warm sunshine and a drying wind in February can wipe away weeks of December gloom. As we get older we realise that the days are more precious and half-moments of intense joy are more valuable than jewels.

Making this garden has so far taken us over ten years of hard work and has become completely interwoven with our history. But in the end the most exciting time of all is always the shining here and now.

Index

Page numbers in *italic* refer to the illustrations